SO FAR
FROM HOME

Other Books by Margaret J. Wheatley

Walk Out Walk On: A Learning Journey into Communities Daring to Live the Future Now, coauthored with Deborah Frieze

Perseverance

Finding Our Way: Leadership for an Uncertain Time

Turning to One Another: Simple Conversations to Restore Hope to the Future

A Simpler Way, coauthored with Myron Kellner-Rogers

Leadership and the New Science: Discovering Order in a Chaotic World

SO FAR FROM HOME

lost and found in our
brave new world

MARGARET J. WHEATLEY

Berrett–Koehler Publishers, Inc.
San Francisco
a BK Life book

Berrett-Koehler Publishers, Inc.
235 Montgomery, Suite 650
San Francisco, CA 94104-2916
Tel: (415) 288-0260   Fax: (415) 362-2512   www.bkconnection.com

Ordering Information

Quantity sales. Special discounts are available on quantity purchases by corporations, associations, and others. For details, contact the "Special Sales Department" at the Berrett-Koehler address above.

Individual sales. Berrett-Koehler publications are available through most bookstores. They can also be ordered directly from Berrett-Koehler: Tel: (800) 929-2929; Fax: (802) 864-7626; www.bkconnection.com

Orders for college textbook/course adoption use.
Please contact Berrett-Koehler: Tel: (800) 929-2929; Fax: (802) 864-7626.

Orders by U.S. trade bookstores and wholesalers.
Please contact Ingram Publisher Services, Tel: (800) 509-4887; Fax: (800) 838-1149; E-mail: customer.service@ingram publisherservices.com; or visit www.ingrampublisherservices.com/Ordering for details about electronic ordering.

Berrett-Koehler and the BK logo are registered trademarks of Berrett-Koehler Publishers, Inc.

Printed in the United States of America

Berrett-Koehler books are printed on long-lasting acid-free paper. When it is available, we choose paper that has been manufactured by environmentally responsible processes. These may include using trees grown in sustainable forests, incorporating recycled paper, minimizing chlorine in bleaching, or recycling the energy produced at the paper mill.

Production management: Michael Bass Associates
Book and cover designer: Canace Pulfer
Cover photograph: Margaret J. Wheatley

Cataloging information is available from the Library of Congress, catalog record no. 2012025518.
ISBN 978-1-60994-536-7

First Edition

17 16 15 14   10 9 8 7 6 5 4 3 2

DEDICATION

For all of us who aspire to be warriors for the human spirit, and for those whose needs and suffering summon us to be brave.

For Yava Rukshi, whose protective and challenging presence and beautiful home provided the container for this book to take form.

For my teachers who proclaim the teachings, radiate confidence, and illuminate the way of discipline. I do not have words to express my gratitude and devotion: The Vidyadhara Chögyam Trungpa and Pema Chödrön.

CONTENTS

Part III
Lost: Opening to the world as it is

Part IV
Found: Discovering gentleness, decency, bravery

HOME IS

The source of vivid memories for a place we've never been

the yearning for return to a place we've yet to find

the sense of true belonging

when we know that we've been found

the confidence to journey through this life.

—Margaret J. Wheatley

AN INVITATION TO YOU AS READER

I wrote this book for you if you offer your work as a contribution to others, wherever and whatever that work might be. And if you now find yourself feeling more exhausted, frustrated, overwhelmed, and sad while also experiencing moments of joy, belonging, and increased resolve to continue your work.

This book can restore your clarity, energy, and enthusiasm for your work if you take time with it and read it slowly.

This book cannot serve you if you skim, scan, scroll, or flip through its pages hunting for a few good ideas.

This book intends to provoke and disturb, to console and affirm you. These strong responses require time and reflection.

This book explores how this brave new world—so difficult and destructive of our good work—emerged from complex causes and conditions. Complexity takes time to understand.

This book invites you to choose a new role for yourself so that you might better serve the people, causes, and places important to you. Conscious choices take time to discern.

This book calls upon skills not common these days, such as thinking, sense making, pattern recognition, reflection. These skills return when we free our minds of distraction and enter the quiet space of contemplation.

I invite you to explore this book slowly so that it might illuminate and clarify your path going forward.

May this book benefit you so that you might benefit many others.

Meg Wheatley

AN INVITATION TO WARRIORSHIP

Most cultures identify this as a dark time, an age of destruction, the end of a cycle or the end of times. And most cultures have the tradition of warriors, an elite class entrusted with defending the faith, the culture, or the kingdom. Warriors undergo rigorous training and display great courage; their valiant acts live on in stories that inspire people to maintain the faith and strive to be courageous.

For many years now, I have been inspired, motivated, and comforted by a prophecy that comes from Tibetan Buddhism of impending darkness and the summoning of the warriors. Although this word *warrior* has heavy connotations of force and aggression, it means something very different in Tibetan culture. The Tibetan word for warrior, *pawo*, means one who is brave, one who vows never to use aggression. I practice for this kind of warriorship in a lineage based on the prophecy of the Shambhala warriors. My personal vow is to refrain, as best I can, from adding to the aggression and fear of this time. Shambhala was an ancient kingdom of wise and conscious people, ruled by enlightened kings. (My Tibetan teacher places it in current-day Afghanistan.[1] Others believe it is not a physical place but a description of our awakened minds.) The people of Shambhala were unusual in that they had no anxiety. Free from fear, they were able to create an enlightened society.

The prophecy of the Shambhala warriors comes from an ancient time, speaking across a vast distance to our present one: "There comes a time when all life on Earth is in danger. Great barbarian powers have arisen. Although these powers spend their wealth in preparations to annihilate one another, they have much in common: weapons of unfathomable destructive power, and technologies that lay waste our world. In this era, when the future of sentient life hangs by the frailest of threads, the kingdom of Shambhala emerges."[2]

You cannot tell who these warriors are by their appearance; they look like normal people doing regular jobs. They are, however, extremely well armed. Their "weapons" are powerful. compassion and insight. Well trained in their use, they go into the corridors of power to dismantle the beliefs and behaviors that are destroying life.

When I first heard this prophecy, I was very moved by the description of the warriors—already inside the halls of power, knowledgeable about the inner workings of these systems, perfectly positioned to discern the causes and conditions that had led to the descent into darkness. These warriors would not succumb to aggression or be paralyzed by fear. They would know where best to use their skillful means of compassion and insight.

Perhaps you see yourself in this description or are curious to investigate what it might mean. This is my invitation to you, to all of us who are in these systems of power, who know their inner workings, who know they cannot be rescued or reversed. We are free to choose a new role for ourselves, to transform our grief, outrage, frustration, and exhaustion into the skills of insight and compassion, to serve this dark time as warriors for the human spirit.

PART I

NEW WORLD

Oh brave new world!
That has such people in it!

SHAKESPEARE, *THE TEMPEST*

I

SEEING WHAT IS

I'm sitting on the banks of the Virgin River in Zion National Park, my favorite place on the planet. The river is confidently, casually flowing through this magnificent canyon that it has been carving out for about two million years.

The canyon has created one of Earth's most sacred places. It has been a dry winter, so the river is low, ambling peacefully along. I've been here at other times when it's fierce, flooding, destructive. Next time I'm back it will be different again.

I've learned a lot from rivers, starting with the teacher stream I wrote about in *Leadership and the New Science*. That lovely mountain stream taught me about process structures, things that have clear identity and intention yet constantly adapt to circumstances and conditions, changing their form as needed. Streams take many forms yet never lose their way, which is unerringly to the ocean. Along the way, they create magnificent canyons, wreak terrible destruction, provide sustenance to farms and communities, provide pleasure and pain to those who live along their banks. This is the pattern of life—changing, adapting, creating and destroying.

The Hopi Native American elders describe this time—our time—as a river flowing now very fast, great, and swift. They warn us not to hold on to the shore, the place of security and old ways, because those who do "will be torn apart and suffer greatly." They encourage us to push off into the middle of the river and to keep our heads above water.[3]

These river images, even the most turbulent ones, no longer describe this time for me. I need a more violent image of disruption and dread to describe what I'm seeing and how I'm feeling. It is Yeats' dark vision that speaks to me, written in 1919 in the troubled years after the First World War:

> Things fall apart; the centre cannot hold;
>
> Mere anarchy is loosed upon the world,
>
> The blood-dimmed tide is loosed, and everywhere
>
> The ceremony of innocence is drowned;

A Confession of Innocence

Many of us—certainly I'd describe myself in these terms—were anxiously engaged in "the ceremony of innocence." We didn't think we were innocents, but we were. We thought we could change the world. We even believed that, with sufficient will and passion, we could "create a world," one that embodied our aspirations for justice, equality, opportunity, peace, a world where, in Paulo Freire's terms, "it would be easier to love." (The gifted publisher of this and all my books, Berrett-Koehler, aspires "To create a world that works for all.") This vision, this hope, this possibility motivated me for most of my life. It still occasionally seduces me into contemplating what might be the next project, the next collaboration, the next big idea that could turn this world around. But I'm learning to resist the temptation.

This is not a book that contemplates what we might do next, what we've learned from all our efforts, where we might put our energy and experience in order to create positive change. I no longer believe that we can save the world. Powerful, life-destroying dynamics have been set in motion that cannot be stopped. We're on a disastrous course with each other and with the planet. We've lost track of our best human qualities and forgotten the real sources of satisfaction, meaning and joy.

This book was born from my clarity that greed, self-interest and coercive power are destroying the very life force of this planet. I don't know whether such destruction is intentional or not, but I observe it happening everywhere. I was hit in the face with this while in South Africa in November 2011. South Africa is the country of my heart, always teaching me about the depths of human experience. I've been working there since 1995 and this was my fourteenth visit. In the years of Nelson Mandela, hope was palpable. Everyone seemed to be starting projects to tackle huge social problems, eager to work with others to create the New South Africa. They understood the complexity of all the issues, they knew it was "a long walk to freedom,"[4] and they had great faith in their future.

But now, for many reasons, hope is hard to find and the good people who have created successful projects and built effective non-government organizations (NGOs) are exhausted and demoralized. They keep doing their work, but it's now a constant struggle. They struggle for funds, they struggle with inept, corrupt bureaucracy, they struggle with the loss of community and the rise of self-interest, they struggle with the indifference of the newly affluent. The dream of a new nation of possibility, equality, and justice has fallen victim to the self-serving behaviors of those with power.

Please do not think this is only true in South Africa. It's happening everywhere, as you may have noticed.

Indestructible Motivation

Yet I have not set out to write a book that increases our despair. Quite the contrary. My intention is that we do our work with greater resolve and energy, with more delight and confidence, even as we understand that it won't turn this world around. Our work is essential; we just have to hold it differently. This was beautifully described by Václav Havel, leader of the Velvet Revolution, the poet-playwright who then became president of the new Czech Republic: "Hope is not the conviction that something will turn out well, but the certainty that something makes sense, regardless of how it turns out."[5]

How do we find this deep confidence that, independent of results, our work is the right work for us to be doing? How do we give up needing hope to be our primary motivator? How do we replace hope of creating change with confidence that we're doing the right work?

Hope is such a dangerous source of motivation. It's an ambush, because what lies in wait is hope's ever-present companion, fear: the fear of failing, the despair of disappointment, the bitterness and exhaustion that can overtake us when our best, most promising efforts are rebuked, undone, ignored, destroyed. As someone commented, "Expectation is premeditated disappointment."

My great teachers these days are people who no longer need hope in order to do their work, even though their projects and organizations began with bright, hope-filled dreams. As "the blood-dimmed tide" of greed, fear, and oppression drowns out their voices and washes away their good work, they become more committed to their work, not because it will succeed, but just because it is right for them to be doing it. I watch their inner struggles and bouts with despair, but mostly what I notice is their perseverance and confidence. They see how bad it is, they know it is getting worse, they realize their work won't create the changes they have worked hard for all these years. Yet they continue to do their work because they know it is theirs to do. Sometimes they say, "I can't not do this." Other times they ask, "What else would I be doing if not this?"

These brave people are true warriors. Seeing as clearly as they can, hearts as open as they can bear, they keep doing their work. They know how systems of power work and they try to discern wise actions. Though in frequent battles with politicians, leaders and bureaucrats, they strive to keep their hearts open and not to succumb to anger and aggression. Work is filled with constant challenges, and they know there will be many more.

Perhaps you see yourself in this description. Or perhaps you still rely on the hope that it's possible to save the world.

2

DO YOU WANT TO SAVE THE WORLD?

I use this rather dramatic phrase of "saving the world" to get your attention and also to make a point.

You may not hold your work in such grandiose terms; you may be working hard to create change within one community, one organization, or for one cause. You haven't been contemplating how to change the whole world, just working on the small piece in front of you. But many of us harbor the hope that if we do a good job and have evidence of our results, our work will spread and create change beyond our initial project or place. For me, such hope places you in the category of saving the world.

A few questions to see whether you fit in this category:

~ When you've discovered a process or project that works well, do you assume that others will be interested in how you achieved your success?
~ Do you present your good results, with supporting evidence, and assume that this will convince others to adopt your model?
~ Do you sometimes imagine how your good work could be taken up by enough other people that it goes to scale, creating change far beyond your own sphere of influence?

~ Have you presented your work at conferences or meetings hoping to have this kind of impact?

These hopes and dreams are quite normal in my experience, and it's hard to let them go. But they're based on an assumption of rational human behavior—that leaders are interested in what works—that has not proven true. Time and again, innovators and their highly successful projects are ignored, denied or pushed aside, even in the best of times. In this dark era, this is even more true.

If we choose to stay in our work and claim the role of warrior, our aspiration changes in a dramatic way—we give up needing anyone else to adopt our good work. We focus on where we are, who we're with, what we're doing within our specific sphere of influence. We do our work with even greater focus and determination: and we abandon dreams of influencing anybody else. This is what I mean by giving up saving the world.

But we do not give up our work. We act with greater clarity and courage once freed from oppressive ambition. And we cheerfully choose a new role, transforming from savior to warrior.

Warriors for the Human Spirit
The subject of this book is warriorship. I want to encourage us to claim this role for ourselves, to be warriors for the human spirit, people brave enough to refrain from adding to the fear and aggression of this time. This is no easy task, not to meet aggression with aggression, to consciously choose to stay out of fear and support others to do the same, to quell the anxiety and anger that erupts so reflexively and choose for peace. Of course it's hard—what isn't these days? I just want to be struggling for the right things.

As I've claimed this role for myself, I'm learning that the capacities and skills we most need—patience, compassion, discernment, effectiveness, courage—are available to us if we can see the world honestly and not flee from its harshness. This is ancient wisdom, expressed clearly by the Tibetan Buddhist master Chögyam Trungpa:

We cannot change the world as it is,

but by opening ourselves to the world as it is,

we may find that gentleness, decency and bravery are available—

not only to us but to all human beings.[6]

I've been contemplating this teaching for a few years, enticed by its description of a path that is both paradoxical and straightforward. If we fully accept the world as it is—in all its harsh realities—then we can develop the very qualities we need to be in that world and not succumb to that harshness. We find our courage, morality, and gentle, non-aggressive actions by clear seeing and acceptance. As we accept what is, we become people who stand in contrast to what is, freed from the aggression, grasping and confusion of this time. With that clarity, we can contribute things of eternal importance no matter what's going on around us—how to live exercising our best human qualities, and how to support others to discover these qualities in themselves.

Archbishop Desmond Tutu, whose work and faith led him to confront and transcend the most dehumanizing violence and degradation of the human spirit, proclaims that this is a moral universe. Martin Luther King, Jr. noted, "The arc of the universe is long but it tends towards justice."[7] I honor the valiant warriorship of these two great men and hold their lives with reverence. Yet I don't need their statements to be true in order to claim my own warriorship. Perhaps the world progresses slowly but inexorably toward justice and morality. But the evidence is certainly mixed.

I personally aspire to be so free of hope and fear that I don't need some future far-off progress to commit to my work right now. It doesn't matter which way history moves. What matters is now: how we live, work and create together in this very moment, relying on and cultivating our best human qualities, creating meaning by how we are together in the present moment. Perhaps this contributes to the arc of history that Dr. King describes, but who knows? I've let go of my need to influence the course of history. I've chosen between two paths: one path is offering me meaning, strength, and contentment; one path lures me into further exhaustion and despair. At least that's been my experience. I invite you to explore this for yourself in the coming pages.

3

NEW MAPS FOR
LOST PEOPLE

For many years I've thought of myself as a kind of cartographer. This was the primary image in Leadership and the New Science, *where I described the discoveries of new science as lands rich in possibility, dimly seen, awaiting our voyages of discovery.*

I thought of us as brave explorers, eager to learn more about the world described by new science—a world of unending relationships, infinite creativity, and order for free.

When I drew those first maps in 1992, I assumed my job was quite straightforward. My task was to provide just enough detail of these lands of bright vision and possibility so that people would begin their own explorations. And a good number of people did; their explorations and experiments manifested in many forms, from new approaches to leadership, to healthy communities, to organization-wide transformations. And today, as the world becomes ever more chaotic, more people are becoming interested, if not desperate, to find ways to lead in this turbulence. But in spite of our courage, dedication, and very hard work, we're now lost in a world where we don't want to be. What happened to that bright new world that seemed so close at hand only a few years ago?

When hikers are lost in the wilderness, as you'll read in Chapter 8, "Are We Lost?" they cling to their old maps far too long, driving themselves to exhaustion and despair, threatening their very survival. Unable to acknowledge that they don't know where they are, they grasp wildly at any scrap of information that would confirm their old maps. But they *are* lost. And they need new maps.

We, too, are lost in the wilderness of a brave new world, a global culture whose values and practices are completely opposite to what we set out to create. We didn't intend to be here—we were working for a very different destination. But here we are and, like all lost people, we need first to acknowledge that we are truly lost, so that we stop relying on outdated maps. If we can stop our frantic activity and see this new world clearly, we will be able to create new maps to make our way forward.

A Book of New Maps
This book offers a set of new maps. They are not the only ones that could be drawn, but they are the ones I felt compelled to lay out, based on my training as a systems thinker and my observations from being out in the world with people these many years. Here you will find maps of three different kinds. The first are topographical, in that they describe the characteristics and features, the terrain of this brave new world. These maps are in Part II: "Home: We Cannot Change the Way the World Is."

The second are quite different. They are systems maps, describing the interplay of life's dynamics with human values and behavior, complex interactions that gave rise to what has emerged. I think of these systems maps as charts of the pre-vailing currents that carried us here against our will. They are in Part III: "Lost: Opening to the World as It Is."

The last maps are personal, describing what is required to do our work once we commit to walking the warrior's path. These are in Part IV: "Found: Discovering Gentleness, Decency, and Bravery."

To entice you to begin your exploration, here is a bit more detail of the maps you'll find in each part.

Home: We Cannot Change the Way the World Is
I begin by exploring the capacities of life that have created our wondrous home planet. I describe how three of life's most powerful dynamics are revealing themselves at present, both in the new sciences and in the current global culture.

Chapter 4 "Everything Comes from Somewhere"

Chapter 5 "Emergence: Surprised by Newness"

Chapter 6 "Identity: The Logic of Change"

Chapter 7 "Relationships: Endlessly Entangled"

Lost: Opening to the World as It Is
My intent is for us to see as clearly as possible what's going on in our world in all its harsh details so that we can recognize how lost we truly are. Only if we acknowledge that we are lost can we begin to become unlost. These systems maps describe the complexity of factors and their interactions that have led us to where we are today.

Chapter 8   "Are We Lost?"

Chapter 9   "All-Consuming Selves"

Chapter 10 "Distracted Beyond Recall"

Chapter 11 "Controlling Complexity"

Found: Discovering Gentleness, Decency, and Bravery

Here I describe the essentials of warriorship, beginning with our unassailable faith in people. I offer several different reflections and practices for how we can practice our new role as warriors: how we develop our two "weapons" of compassion and insight; how we stay together on the path without a goal; and how we discover the place of right work, free from hope and fear.

Chapter 12 "A Prophecy of Warriors"

Chapter 13 "Choosing for the Human Spirit"

Chapter 14 "Warriors at Work"

Chapter 15 "No Hope No Fear"

The book concludes with a guide for warriors and a parable:

"A Path for Warriors"

"A Dream of Warriors"

Wanted: Fearless Readers

I feel it necessary to both warn and encourage you as you begin to read this book. Seeing what is, in all its harshness, is not a pleasant experience. Every time I reread my own writing, I can easily move into despair and overwhelm. So I'm very sensitive to what I'm inviting you into and the emotions you may encounter as you read Part II, "Home," and Part III, "Lost."

But I don't end our journey there. I'm asking you to walk through the darkness of this time so that together we can discover the light of clarity and energy for the work we choose to do. The journey of this book ends with Part IV,

"Found," where I describe practices for us warriors that can inspire, sustain, and enliven us for the journey ahead. So if you feel your steps faltering as you encounter how dark it really is, please keep going until you reach Part IV and discover the light that beckons us on.

PART II

HOME

We cannot change the way
the world is

4

EVERYTHING COMES FROM SOMEWHERE

*I've spent many years in a love affair with life.
My passion has increased as I've explored the new
sciences and worked out in the world for decades
with a great variety of people.*

How could I help but fall in love with the planet's excessive, exuberant creativity and with people's generosity and care for one another? I haven't kept my love affair secret. In my writings and teachings, I've encouraged us to notice that life is a good partner, willingly offering us the capacities we need. Life gives us a world rich in potential, where every new relationship offers us new qualities and skills. Life gives us a world of "order for free,"[8] capable of organizing itself, not from oppressive control but from inner coherence. Life gives us unending, incessant creativity, eager to create newness wherever it can, mostly to fill a need or adapt to changing conditions, but sometimes, I firmly believe, just for the fun of it (think of tropical fish).

As with all true loves, I also feel overwhelming sadness to see how we have rebuffed the planet, failing to notice or choosing to ignore what life so easily offers. Instead of partnering, we've taken over, arrogantly assuming that we know best, that we can force the planet to comply with our rules and needs. Of course this has failed; as ecologists often remind us, "Nature bats last."

I've also spent most of my life exploring the power of possibilities, of how great visions and causes inspire us to do the impossible. As a young woman, I took Robert Kennedy's statement to heart: "There are those that look at things the way they are, and ask why? I dream of things that never were, and ask why not?"

Yet now, I need to ask, "Why?" I want to know how we ended up with this life-destroying world that nobody seems to want. I want to know why the forces of destruction have taken over the forces of creation, why our hard work and years of effort haven't created the world we want. I want to discern the reasons, the causes and conditions, that led us so far from home.

Many people I talk with are despairing and confused, unable to comprehend how so much could have gone wrong in the world. Whenever we don't understand the causes of our suffering, our despair intensifies. It is easy to feel victims of randomness. But this is not a random universe—everything comes from somewhere. There are good science-based explanations of how we got to where we don't want to be. Life has continued to create change through its well-known processes.

We need to get reacquainted with our home planet if we are to understand how we landed up here; we need to see as clearly as possible how life's reliable dynamics interacted with human will to emerge as this life-destroying mess. With such clarity, we can develop insight and discernment. We can wisely choose right action, those actions that make sense in the present circumstance. Without discernment, we act from blind hope, not from clear seeing.

We push on, believing that with just greater effort, more passion and better networking, we will force the world to change for the better.

I feel strongly that we are misperceiving both our own and the planet's capacities. We need to understand how we got here, otherwise we'll continue to exhaust ourselves to the point of collapse. It's happening all around us—people getting ill, resigning, withdrawing into cynicism and bitterness. We have to stop this waste of wonderful humans. We have to realize that we're exhausted because we are struggling to accomplish what can never be accomplished. And then blaming ourselves and each other for our failures.

In "Home," I describe three of life's most transforming dynamics, hoping to illuminate how we got to this current dark reality. Many of the science themes will be familiar to you if you've read any of my books or articles. What is different now is how I'm using the science. When I first presented discoveries from new science, I was excited that they revealed new maps for working and organizing that would unleash human capacity. If we understood how this planet functions, we would be able to create healthy organizations and communities. But that hasn't happened. Now I feel compelled to use science to explain why these destructive cycles arose, why they cannot be stopped.

My purpose, as I will keep repeating, is not to add to our despair. My intention is to increase our clarity so that we might discern wise action. We cannot change the way the world is, but by opening to the world as it is, we can discover how to be warriors for the human spirit.

5

EMERGENCE: SURPRISED BY NEWNESS

This troubled, troubling world that we've been working so hard to change for all these years is a world that has emerged.

This is a seemingly innocuous statement, but it has profound implications for us and our work. This world did not materialize from plans, conspiracies, or randomness: it came from life's process of creating new and more complex systems. Emergence is how change happens on this planet, but it is one of the most difficult things to comprehend for those of us trained to think of change as incremental. At least this has been my personal experience in teaching it for many years now. Emergence is where old and new science diverge absolutely, never to be reconciled. However, once we understand emergence, it gives us the capacity to see our world more clearly and to choose wisely where to invest our energy and heart.

Reductionist science still dominates our thinking. Any complex phenomenon is viewed as a machine built from many separate parts. Puzzles are a good way to explore the difference between reductionist and emergent thinking, and it is a common image in use these days. People say they're searching for the missing piece of an organizational puzzle or have just found it. I've been to more than one conference where the name tags were in the shape of puzzle pieces, with the message that "Everyone has a piece of the puzzle." (I think this was meant to be inspiring.)

Reductionist science wants to understand the puzzle's finished form—say, a breathtaking picture of a beautiful mountain scene—by taking it apart, disassembling what may have taken days or weeks to put together. Each piece would be carefully examined to discover the properties that gave rise to the beautiful picture. It is assumed that there is no difference between a completed puzzle and the pile of pieces in a box. The visual experience of the whole—its beauty—can be understood by studying each individual piece in isolation.

I hope this example makes clear the ludicrous assumptions of reductionist thinking. But before you shake your head in disbelief that science could be so stupid, think about all the times you've either used the puzzle image or spent hours trying to "puzzle out" a difficult problem by taking it apart, focusing on just one cause or one particular person. This is how we've been trained—we take things apart to understand them, with little or no thought that we're dealing with emergence, the creation of new properties that do not resemble the parts and that therefore can never be understood by dissection.

Emergence continues to startle scientists, most recently in genetics. Do you remember the Human Genome Project? Begun in 1990 with enormous hoopla and $3 billion of U.S. federal funds, the intent was "to gain knowledge of the human" by mapping our 23,000-plus human genes (involving billions of biochemicals). We were promised lives free from degenerative diseases, perhaps even the end of ageing, all from identifying which genes were responsible for what. The mapping was highly complex, requiring enormous high-speed computing, but the basic theory was simple and mechanistic. Genes were switches— once their functions were identified, they could simply be turned on and off to do what we wanted. Although mapping continues (old ways die slowly), the critical discovery from the Genome Project was that genes are *not* simple switches. DNA is a set of complex relationships of proteins and other biochemicals that interact with genes to create inheritance. Heredity is the result of multiple interactions, an emergent phenomenon. (There's more to read about this in Chapter 6, "Identity: The Logic of Change.")

Nothing Changes One Thing at a Time
Emergence is how life changes, never from just a single cause, but from a complexity of many causes and parts interacting. Life is messy, a reality we continue to deny. Reductionism, being so simple, is much more appealing; I think this is why we continue to use it. We may not realize that we're doing our work from a reductionist mindset, but anytime we focus on a single factor, or search for simple cause and effect, we are. I see it in so many well-intended projects that work to change a category of behavior, such as violence or addiction, yet don't seem to account for the complexity of causes and contexts that came together to emerge as that behavior. For example, I know many wonderful people, including the Dalai Lama, working hard to reduce children's aggression—bullying, physical fights, aggressive language—by teaching them how to work with their anger, how to be more compassionate, how to talk with one another. This work is extremely important as children are, indeed, becoming more violent. But what about the larger cultural context in which our children grow up? What about the bullying and violent language common now in children's movies? What about the increasingly aggressive language we use to describe everyday things?

(How many emails did you shoot today?) What about hateful political rhetoric? Just after the horrific Columbine school massacre, I recall going into a garden store and noticing how many fertilizer and pest products had the word *kill* on their labels.

Anytime we focus on discrete behaviors or work to create cultural change by focusing on individuals, we're bound to be defeated by emergence, just as geneticists were. The world does not change "one person at a time." I'd like to abolish that phrase—now applied to just about everything—because it misrepresents how change happens. To understand emergence, we need to shift our attention from the one-at-a-time to the whole, to the varying dynamics and influences that are clearly visible in individuals but that do not originate in the individual.

Individuals *do* play a fundamental role in contributing to the birth of an emergent system. At the beginning, each part is acting in isolation, making decisions based on its own needs. But as separate elements start to connect with one another, emergence begins. Individual actions that were insignificant start to have new consequences because they are interconnected. At some point, a system will emerge with new and surprising properties that, from that point on, will profoundly influence the behaviors of the individual parts. What emerges is always surprising because it is so different from the parts that created it. You could examine the puzzle pieces under the world's best micron microscope and never find any hint of the puzzle's beauty. Capacities, behaviors, norms emerge that are truly new. They simply do not exist until the system emerges. They are qualities of the system, not of its parts.

Working with Emergence

As strange as this may seem to our reductionist minds, emergence is an everyday experience. Anytime we cook or bake something using more than a single ingredient, we are relying on emergence for flavor. The separate ingredients of eggs, flour, butter, and chocolate never predict the deliciousness of a chocolate chip cookie. And anyone who's been in a choir or band knows the reliable thrill of emergence. Separate voices and instruments come together to create something that didn't, that couldn't, exist had people not joined together. No matter how beautiful one person's voice, it doesn't predict or even contain the harmony of a choir. Jazz players have to trust emergence more than most musicians—jazz wouldn't exist without the surprise of what emerges when it all comes together and transcends individual virtuosity. There's a Sufi teaching I've used often: You think because two and two are four that you understand. But you must also understand *and*.

I know of many people doing change work who are consciously using emergence as their theory of change. They work from an "emergent design" rather than a strategic plan, meaning they have a clear intent, take the first actions, then see what's needed next. Working this way requires a great deal of awareness, constantly curious to see how the larger system is interacting with our project, what other dynamics are in play, how people are reacting. If we're really good, we take in as much feedback as possible and use it to figure out what to do next. We don't use this feedback to find consensus or to please everyone. It is information about the system that can give us invaluable insight into how to achieve the outcomes we need, taking into account the larger context that includes other players and other demands. If we operate from this level of awareness, we become more skillful as we do the work and increase our chances of success. And if we don't succeed, we will understand the multiple causes and conditions that led to our defeat. And hopefully we won't beat up on ourselves or our colleagues as the single cause of our failure.

Great performances, delicious cookies, successful change projects can never be deconstructed to reveal the real secret of their success. In an emergent world, nothing useful gets revealed by dissection. You can't work backward; you can't hope to either re-create something wonderful or change something bad by becoming reductionist, by focusing on the parts. Specific individuals can never take the credit or the blame—it's impossible to differentiate individual from group contributions. We continue to do this, of course, because we are so well trained in analysis and breaking things into parts, and also because there are more than enough egos that want to take the credit.

Emergence is a process whereby interactions create something new and different that cannot be changed. Once something has emerged, it's here to stay. The only way to create something different is to start over, to begin again.

I remember the conversation I had with Myron Rogers, as we were writing *A Simpler Way,* in which we realized this truth about emergence. Once something is, we can't work backward to change it. We were out walking and I remember we both stopped dead in our tracks, taking in the implications of this for our work; we'd each built successful consulting practices on the usual, parts-focused approach to change.

Emergence demands a different relationship with life, where we're curious, open, alert. The only thing we can predict is that life will surprise us. We can't see what is coming until it arrives, and once something has emerged, we have to work with what is. We have to be flexible and willing to adapt—we can't keep pushing ahead, blustering on with our now outdated plans and dreams. And it doesn't help to deny what has emerged. We need to be present and willing to accept this new reality. This is what it truly means to work with emergence.

Absurd Heroism
As change agents, activists, concerned citizens, caring human beings, we are attempting to change a global culture that has emerged. How many people on the planet are happy with what's going on? Scarcely any. Most of us are appalled by the aggression, materialism, and greed now so commonplace. We know this global culture has destroyed diversity and community; we see how it seduces youth everywhere to seek satisfaction in material objects; we witness how polarized we've become, how many enemies there are now to fear; we know people and families devastated by wars, natural disasters, and economic collapse. We speak out against corporate power, the deterioration of democracy, the loss of equity and opportunity, poverty, diseases, the annihilation of species and cultures.

We *do* notice what's going on, with sadness and despair. But then we go back to our work, still believing that if we focus on our part, if we fix this and that one at a time, that we will be able to change the way things are. We work harder; we amplify the importance of our cause; we intensify our efforts. We know the world must change—it simply must. We renew our conviction that we will be the ones to change what has emerged.

Well, we can't. The global culture, with all its tragedies and injustices, is an emergent phenomenon. We have to accept this terrifying fact. It came to be from the convergence of many forces and now possesses characteristics that weren't there until it emerged. It has become a world where the values of greed, self-interest, and oppressive power emerged at a global scale and now supersede all other values. Many of us, most of us, don't want it to be this way. We still aspire to work from values of justice, community, compassion, love. And we need to keep on with this, absolutely. But no matter how well we embody these values, no matter how important our work is, we have to hold it differently.

We will not change what has emerged. We are starting over, basing our work on values and practices that are distinctively countercultural, so outside the norm that most people can't understand what we're doing. We need to continue to persevere in our radical work, experimenting with how we can work and live together to evoke human creativity and caring. Only time will tell whether our efforts contribute to a better future. We can't know this, and we can't base our work or find our motivation from expecting to change this world.

Dark Nights of the Soul
Although I write these words as simple declarative statements, I do not underestimate how difficult they are to accept. It has taken me many years and several dark nights of the soul to come to terms with what is going on. Nowadays we label dark nights as depression, but in spiritual traditions, this descent into darkness is recognized as the journey into greater meaning. Dark nights are also excellent examples of how chaos works to create more capacity; like all living systems, we first have to fall apart before

we can figure out how to reorganize ourselves to fit the new environment.[9] This is the role of despair—it causes us to fall apart. In the darkness, we lose all sense of meaning, and this is always an extremely painful and isolating experience. But then, with timing not of our choosing, we find we have come out of the dark, able to once again find meaning and purpose for our lives. I've asked many people how they feel once they have passed through a dark night. They report, and this is my experience also, that they feel stronger and more confident. Having passed through the refiner's fire, they trust themselves to deal with whatever life challenges them with next.

We need to feel despair that we cannot change the world. It is appropriate and essential that we do so. And we need to enter into the darkness, because it is the entry point for transformation. From my own experience with dark nights, I know that energy, strength and confidence become available the other side of despair. Having personally made this journey many times, abandoning my savior tendencies, I am eager for you to discover this place as well. It saddens me to see how many are still locked down by the belief that if they just work a little harder, if they just collaborate better or build a bigger network, if they just develop a new approach, they'll turn the world around. Can we please abandon these self-destructive beliefs? Can we have faith that capacity, strength and delight are available to us the other side of darkness?

Consider Sisyphus. As described in both Greek and Roman mythology, Sisyphus was condemned by the gods to an eternity of futile and hopeless labor. He had to roll a rock to the top of a mountain, only to watch it tumble back down from its own weight and the natural force of gravity. Then he would roll it to the top again. Forever. The French existentialist philosopher Albert Camus wrote an essay about absurd heroism and the despair it caused entitled "The Myth of Sisyphus."

Sisyphus had no choice—he had been condemned by the gods. But we do have choice. We can notice the price we're paying for our absurd heroism, for believing that it's up to us. I hear so many people who want to take at least partial responsibility for this mess. Somewhat piously, as if summoning us to accountability, they say, "We need to accept responsibility that we created this" or "We created it, so we can change it." No we didn't. And no we can't. We participated with innumerable other players and causes and this is what emerged. We can't take credit for it, we can't blame ourselves, and we can't put the burden of change on us. We're not Sisyphus, condemned to a fate of absurd heroism.

If Sisyphus had been a free agent, he would have noticed that gravity was the problem. We have to notice that emergence is the problem, as unchallengeable a force as gravity. Let's fully face the brave new world that has emerged and put down our boulder—the energy-destroying belief that we can change the world. Let us walk away from that mountain of despair-inducing failures and focus instead on the people in front of us, our colleagues, communities and families. Let us work together to embody the values that we treasure, and not worry about creating successful models that will transform other people. Let us focus on transforming ourselves to be little islands of good caring people, doing right work, assisting where we can, maintaining peace and sanity, people who have learned how to be gentle, decent, and brave as the dark ocean that has emerged continues to storm around us.

6

IDENTITY:
THE LOGIC OF CHANGE

Several years ago, I received a card from a friend that reminded me how life works: "Change is just the way it is." These days, we're becoming more and more aware of this truth.

Think of the words we use to describe this time. Chaotic. Uncertain. Turbulent. Out of control. Relentless. Crazy. Weird. And random is now a common adjective—I often hear people say, "That's so random."

If change is just the way it is on this planet, what's happening now that makes life feel so difficult, so filled with dread? Is it any different than in the past? Or have we just gotten soft, become whiners and complainers?

I believe that change today is profoundly different in volume, intensity and consequence. We have *changed the experience of change* because of global networks of communication. Never before have we been aware of what's happening just about everywhere on the planet. And never before have we been engaged in instantaneous reactions with one another about everything from the trivial to the life changing. The instant messaging nature of communications has changed change, making it appear more random and irrational. We hear of something instantly: "Breaking news! This just in!" Immediately, we're encouraged to blurt out a reaction through Facebook or texts that will be read on news shows. Even though most of us don't understand "the crisis"—why it happened or its implications—instant reactions are often charged with hysteria, outrage, or grief. Everything becomes a big dramatic deal, but only briefly. The media enflame our reactions, then drop coverage. We may vaguely remember there was a crisis, or not. Often I find myself asking someone, "Whatever happened to the crisis in . . . ?"

Life is hard and there are more than enough real crises, but when we can't distinguish real from manufactured ones, change feels overwhelming. We may continue to react on demand, but we stop thinking. We are not interested in exploring reasons or causes. No wonder that life feels so random.

Change Is Never Random
Life is changing constantly, but change is never random. There are always causes and conditions. The reason that living systems change is in order to survive. If their environment shifts, they adapt, figuring out what works in the context of now. They don't do this as isolated individuals but as neighborhoods. Each individual is free to decide how it will change, but individual adaptations only work within the context of community. It's more accurate to think of sense making and adapting as a collective activity, individual creativity within a community. And it's a process that works well to create difference, differentiation, and coherence—billions of species living in a web of "inter-being," as Thich Nhat Hahn describes it. This is our wondrous planet, "A world which gives birth to ever new variety and ever new manifestations of order against a background of constant change,"[10] adapting, experimenting, discovering what works and, ultimately, surprising us with what emerges.

Change never ceases and it always comes, reliably and predictably, from one primary cause: identity. Life's fundamental process of creation is self-organization—a process described in the term itself: there is always *a self* that gets organized. From the boundless opportunities and ingredients available, every living being takes form with the same first act, defining an identity through the creation of a boundary or membrane. This boundary is critical to differentiate what's in and what's out. Inside is what will be used to form this new entity; outside is what will be ignored (though only at the beginning—organisms with impermeable boundaries die). For a new organism or a new organization, the first creative act in life is to establish an identity. Identity becomes the lens to interpret the world and determine responses: what it needs, how it behaves, how it makes decisions.

The Ultimate Paradox
And here is life's ultimate paradox about change: the only reason a living being changes is so it won't have to change. It will do whatever is necessary to preserve itself. All change starts when we become disturbed—something gets our attention. If we choose to respond to this provocation, it will be, literally, in self-defense. We will make any change that we think will save us, even if we need to change so much that we're barely recognizable. We see this paradox every time a person decides to change jobs, leave a relationship, or get treatment for an addiction. In every case, people are choosing to make a radical change, to become someone different, in order to protect who they are. We humans have a special advantage over other species when it comes to making choices about identity— we are conscious beings and can deliberately work with our thoughts and perceptions to change our minds.

There is no more compelling force for change than identity; it is the essential consideration at the beginning, middle, and end of change.

This global culture that we are desperate to transform is a result of the identity-driven nature of change. Random as it feels, there is a deep ordering dynamic at play, that of self making. This world has emerged from what we think we must have in order to protect ourselves and ensure our continued existence. This is how it always is, organizing around a self, but what's new and different is where our identities now originate, where we get the information to organize a self.

Nothing in the World Is Predetermined
Before I describe the self-manufacturing dynamics of this culture and their dark consequences, there are two discoveries in the newest of the new sciences that are especially relevant to identity, that confirm life's never-ending capacity for change.

To hear people talk, you'd think we live in a deterministic universe. How often do you explain your bad tendencies or good talents by attributing it to your genes? How often do you use DNA to describe your organization's behavior? "It's in our DNA" is a common expression these days to describe either good or bad characteristics, but always as if they're predetermined, fixed, incapable of changing.

Or how often do we try to reduce people's expectations of us by insisting, "That's just the way I am" or "You can't teach an old dog new tricks." And are you already explaining problems with memory, concentration, and thinking as unavoidable, determined by your age?

All of these comments describe a universe far different from the one we live in, a world of constant change and unending creativity. Luckily for us, we are discovering that change is true even for what we thought fixed and determinate—our DNA and our brains.

Some of the most exciting developments in science these days are discoveries that the elements in our bodies that we assumed were set for life are, in fact, changing all the time, influenced by what we think and what we do. Developments in two fields, neuroscience and epigenetics, are causing scientists to abandon their highly mechanistic and deterministic models of DNA and the human brain. It's taken a great deal of courage and perseverance on the part of a few pioneering scientists to shift our understanding. As always happens when science threatens the dominant paradigm, the research gets dismissed and sometimes so do the scientists, from their university positions and grants. However, the evidence that has been carefully obtained over several years now makes a strong case against the deadening view of mechanistic science— that life is a process of predetermined deterioration and decay. What these new sciences convincingly demonstrate is that this world of constant creation is going on even inside our skulls and DNA.

Brains Reflect the Lives We Lead
Neuroscientists have abandoned older models of the brain as a complex machine or computer. The brain is now described in terms of its plasticity, as a living organ that keeps changing over the entire course of a life. (The term plasticity was first used in 1890 by William James, the father of experimental psychology. It seems to take about a century for major paradigm shifts—it's also taken nearly

a hundred years for quantum reality to be accepted.) If the human brain suffers injury, it is capable of repairing damaged regions by growing new neurons; if that doesn't work, it will use regions that had performed one task and convert them to function as a replacement for the damaged region. If someone becomes blind from a brain injury, the visual cortex can change its function and dedicate its space to improved hearing. Our brains willingly change, weaving new neural networks so we can continue to experience life. Like everything else in life, brains adapt and change as necessary to meet current conditions.

Even the structure of the brain is more adaptive than any mechanistic model could ever have imagined. Functions such as memory, emotions, thinking, dreaming are not located solely in one particular area of the brain. As one neuroscientist commented, diagrams of which brain regions perform what function should be printed in erasable ink.[11]

Our brains change as we interact with our environment, as we live our lives. Our brains respond to what we do and, perhaps more astonishingly, to what we think. Our thoughts and actions, if repeated even for only brief periods of time, send messages to the brain and the brain responds by creating physical changes that strengthen our capacities in these particular areas. And it doesn't take long for the brain to change. In one experiment, people's brains developed physical changes making them more adept at scanning web pages after practicing one hour a day for just five days.[12]

Our brains differ from person to person because of what we do and what skills we have developed. The motor cortex of violinists has more space dedicated to rapid finger movement. But interestingly, brains can change without us doing any physical effort; they can change because of what we think. The motor cortex also grows in people who never sit down at a piano but who spend time consciously imagining that they are playing the piano. The brain's response to conscious thoughts, not only to actions, is why athletes can prepare successfully for races by visualizing each part of the course in great detail. Our brains, in both the size of different regions and the strength of connections between one area and another, embody the lives we lead and the lives we imagine.

DNA Changes Based on Experience

It is not only our brains that are changed by how we live. The new field of epigenetics is establishing how environmental influences impact heredity. DNA can be changed by what we experience in life; these changes can be passed on to our children, possibly for generations. Epigenetics grew out of the Human Genome Project as researchers developed a new understanding of genes. (See the preceding chapter, "Emergence: Surprised by Newness.") Genes are only one factor in a network of relationships among proteins and other biochemicals. Epigeneticist Richard Frances describes genes not as directors of the play of life but as part of an improvisational ensemble cast.[13] Many more players than genes within DNA affect heredity. Our genetics emerge, like everything else in life, from complex interactions among multiple actors.

Epigenetics has focused attention on such important things as nutrition in pregnant women. Although the baby is in the womb, its future seemingly already determined by genes, what the mother eats and how the mother feels affects the baby's DNA and has a large impact on the future health of the baby—its propensity for diabetes, cancer, weight, depression, and life span. In another study, boys who smoked before puberty, before their sperm were even formed, negatively affected the health of their future offspring, not by changing their genes but by creating other cellular influences on their DNA that were then passed on through their sperm.[14]

If we want to keep using DNA to describe ourselves and our organizations, please let's use it based on this new understanding. DNA is a troupe of actors, improvising genetic changes as we live our lives. A deterministic universe is nowhere to be found. We have the power to determine our futures.

What we do matters. Whether we take care of ourselves, our physical and mental selves, matters. What we engage in, what we think about, matters. Life is right here, willing to create the capacities we need to support us. But we must be the ones to consciously choose those capacities. And by the way, our issues with memory loss, lack of concentration, and attention span are not all age related. They are the result of distraction, as you'll read in Chapter 10, "Distracted Beyond Recall."

The Machinery of Self-Manufacture
These discoveries in new science are quite inspiring—at least I hope you find them so—but they are also very sobering if we contemplate how our current culture's intense, incessant focus on the self must be affecting our brains and DNA.

Throughout history, human identities have been a natural consequence of where people were born—their tribe, community, culture. Who we were was never a question—we naturally learned the ways of our people and participated in our culture, unaware that there were other ways to live. Some cultures went to war against others, some didn't. But successful empires such as the Romans learned that it was easier to rule if those conquered were allowed to maintain their own cultures. Cultural identity is a great cohering influence on people; it binds us together with a shared lens for interpreting life and deciding our actions. It offers stable ground to stand on in the midst of chaos.

Now this has all changed. Identity is still the organizing dynamic—it can't be otherwise. But in our globally connected world, our identities come not from cultural or family traditions, but from marketing departments. It is identity that sells products: if you buy this, you'll look and feel like these beautiful successful people. Magazines and TV shows are filled with identity choices—lifestyles, fashion, home decor, music, films, food, travel—everything is a choice and what we choose tells people who we are. It's common now to describe yourself in terms of what kind of person you are, either a this or a that: "I'm a dog person, not a cat person." In an airport, I overheard a seven-year-old girl ask her nine-year-old sister, "Am I a clothes person or an accessory person?" Without hesitating, her sister instantly replied, "Oh, you're definitely an accessory person."

Teens report how in high school they become experts at writing profiles of themselves, "making a me," as one young man described it, both for social media and college applications.[15] Others reported how stressful it was to fill out the many lists of preferences to create a Facebook profile. They'd spend days agonizing over which music, bands, TV shows, movies to list, and then equally agonize over which order to put them in, sometimes market-testing different lists to see which ones got them "friended" more on Facebook.[16]

Branding now also plays a dominant role in identity creation. What is a brand but a lens intentionally and artfully created by someone trying to influence how we perceive them? And it is not just organizations that brand themselves; so do individuals and politicians. I remember a thirty-something woman telling me how she chose a particular online dating site because it fit her brand. It seems clear to me that this is the era of manufactured identities, made to order by individuals free from any cultural constraints or family ties, changed at will, driven by popularity, and fueled by the lure of materialism. How can these manufactured selves be anything but meaningless? How could they ever commit to long-term relationships or to disciplined, sometimes boring work when they are based on superficial preferences that change on a whim?

Life's basic process of self making has been exploited, first by marketeers, then by individuals trying to find friends. It can't create a coherent system—no neighborhoods where individual decisions are made keeping in mind the collective. Instead, identity needs drive people to seek gratification on their own, independent of any larger context. I describe this march into lonely and meaningless lives in Chapter 9, "All-Consuming Selves."

There is another exploitation of identity making that is wreaking destruction in the world, the polar opposite of individual self manufacturing. It's the cultivation of strong, violent, ethnic, and national identities by those craving political power. Historically, it is a guaranteed strategy for gaining control over people. The leader creates an inspiring definition of who we are, defining us as inherently superior; our superiority gives us the right to take anything we want, no matter the cost; an impermeable boundary is drawn between us and them; we have many enemies and must defend ourselves at all costs, including war.

This use of identity has succeeded over many centuries, and it is here today, in extreme political rhetoric, in increasing polarization, in difference defined as the enemy. And it is here in genocide, terrorism, ethnic cleansing, and the modern weapons of war that deliberately slaughter the innocents, the women and children.

The Values of Global Culture

This is what has emerged, this destructive global culture that nobody wanted. It has emerged from life's primary organizing dynamic—self-organization. Its destructive qualities are a consequence of the values and beliefs that were used to organize both personal and group identities. Self-organization is a process—it has no inherent values, neither good nor bad. But as a process, it uses values as the basis for how to organize. To understand anything that has emerged, it is important to work backward, to deduce the values and beliefs that must have been used to organize this emergent phenomenon. Using this deductive approach, if we look honestly at our current world, the values of this culture become brutally clear—self-interest, greed, power. These values are so very different from what we wanted or what we continue to strive for.

So what do we do? We cannot change this world, as fearsome as it is. It's an emergent phenomenon that will not be changed no matter what we do. Instead, let's make good use of the process of self making, consciously choosing values and beliefs that support meaningful lives and strong community where we are and with those we're with. And in this, life is right here as a good partner. We can use our minds to make conscious choices, knowing that our bodies will respond and create the physical changes necessary to support our choices. If we choose to be warriors for the human spirit, we will develop the capacities we need—gentleness, discernment, bravery, love. As we embody these, we can trust that our brains will strengthen these qualities in us. And who knows how our DNA might be affected!

Or we can continue our Sisyphean behaviors, searching for slightly more manageable boulders. We can develop our capacity for courageous clear-seeing or for absurd heroism. Either way our brains and bodies will be there, changing to support our choices.

7

RELATIONSHIPS: ENDLESSLY ENTANGLED

Albert Einstein described our feelings of separateness as "a kind of optical delusion of consciousness. This delusion is a kind of prison for us, restricting us to our personal desires and affection for a few persons nearest to us.

Our task must be to free ourselves from this prison by widening the circle of understanding and compassion to embrace all living creatures and the whole of nature in its beauty. Nobody is able to achieve this completely, but the striving for such achievement is in itself a part of the liberation and a foundation for inner security."[17]

Yet Einstein struggled his entire life with the entangled nature of this universe, a world where separateness is indeed an illusion. Einstein could not accept what quantum scientists were discovering, a world where seemingly discrete, separate particles acted as one, even when distant from each other. In rejecting this new quantum reality, Einstein labeled it as "spooky action at a distance." First proved in 1964 with Bell's theorem and then in subsequent experiments that continue to this day, quantum reality has been well established. When two separate particles are correlated and then separated, they continue to act as one. If one changes, the other does so instantly, faster than the speed of light. *Entanglement*, the term

used in physics, is now accepted as the defining charac-
teristic of this universe, not just at the quantum level but
at the macroscopic world that we inhabit.[18] "The universe,"
as astronomer Sir James Jeans noted, "begins to look
more like a great thought than like a great machine."[19]

Einstein wasn't the only scientist who, as another scientist
expressed it, was "shaken to the bone" to observe the endlessly entangled nature of reality.[20] It's taken scientists the
entire twentieth century, and an ever-increasing number
of confirming experiments, to let go of their mechanistic
images; separate parts interacting with machine-like predictability in a universe of determinable cause and effect.
As physicist and science commentator Brian Greene
describes it, "The most straightforward reading of the
data is that Einstein was wrong and there can be strange,
weird, and 'spooky' quantum connections between things
over here and things over there. . . . This is an earth-shat-
tering result. This is the kind of result that should take
your breath away."[21]

People Don't Want to Know They're Interconnected
In this global culture built on individualism, people have no
interest in learning about entanglement. Dictionaries too
define it as a problem. Webster's online *The Free Dictionary* defines entanglement as "1. Cause to become twisted
together with or caught in; 2. Involve (someone) in difficulties or complicated circumstances." My Apple computer's dictionary is even more grim: "a complicated or
compromising relationship or situation; an extensive bar-
rier, typically made of interlaced barbed wire and stakes,
erected to impede enemy soldiers or vehicles."

For people who value their right to self-determine, their
freedom to create any self they choose, entanglement is a

huge constriction. Years ago I was part of a small think tank on community preparedness after disasters. I was waxing lyrical about how a disaster shows us how interconnected we are. I will never forget the physicist who leaned across the table at me and said, "Margaret, most people don't want to know they're interconnected." He was absolutely right. Acknowledging interconnectedness is too much of a burden. It requires that we take responsibility for noticing how we affect other people, that we realize how our behaviors and choices impact others, even at a distance. How much easier life is when we don't worry about these multiple layers of impact and just focus on ourselves.

Before the culture of rampant individualism took over, traditional societies had for millennia based their cultures on profound knowledge of entanglement; most cultures, even today, have words and concepts to describe it.[22] In South Africa, the word is *ubuntu*—a rich and complex concept, not easily translated into English. Archbishop Tutu describes it: "Ubuntu means my humanity is caught up, is inextricably bound up, in yours. We belong in a bundle of life. We say, 'a person is a person through other people.' It is not 'I think therefore I am.' It says rather: 'I am human because I belong.'"[23]

Have You Been Spooked by Action at a Distance?
Many of us, even if we are absorbed in our individual selves, have experienced "spooky action at a distance," perhaps even frequently. How many times have you thought of someone, only to have them contact you minutes later? Have you ever experienced a sudden feeling of dread about a loved one, then later learned that something bad happened to them at just that time? When out in nature, have you ever been overcome by a deep sense of belonging, feeling totally connected?

Western science has dismissed these and other experiences—clairvoyance, remote viewing, telepathy—as primitive, superstitious, magical thinking. The National Science Foundation categorized people who have these experiences as either mentally deficient or poorly educated.[24] I've had many of these experiences and continue to both enjoy and rely on these alternative sources of information. It's been easy for me to trust them because I work in many Aboriginal cultures that have never forgotten entanglement. An Australian Aboriginal mother described to me how she would know if her son was in difficulty if her left inner arm began to tingle, just where she had cradled him for so many years. And in both Hinduism and Buddhism there are centuries of reports of teleportation, clairvoyance, and telepathy, skills that are a normal consequence of deep meditation, nothing special.

Einstein was right: we live in a prison created by an optical delusion of separateness. That prison gets strengthened by arrogance, by Western science's willingness to be spooked but their obdurate refusal to be curious about the multitudes of experiences, spanning cultures and centuries, that prove how endlessly entangled we are.

Of course we're entangled. In this universe, relationships are all there is, the fundamental prerequisite for anything to manifest. At the quantum level, an elementary particle isn't visible until it collides with another particle, energy meeting energy. In biology, the concept of a solitary individual doesn't exist—some other discipline made that up. New biology studies the natural world for its ecosystems of interconnectedness, for relationships. One theoretical biologist describes the communication inside living organisms and with other organisms as "a sophisticated ecological system of biochemical dialogue."[25]

Nothing living lives alone. We are all bundles of potentiality that manifest only in relationship, a description of the universe first coined by a quantum theorist.[26] We can't be creative or discover new capacities unless we are in a relationship with something outside our self—another person, an idea, a place or situation. We are not self-made individuals. We are creations of entanglement, becoming and changing through relationships.

Alone Together

This is the nature of our world, and the Internet has contributed to its evolution by creating a global commons intensely rich in relationships. It's obvious that enormous personal creativity has been unleashed because of the Internet's ability to connect us. Distance disappears and people find friendships, romance, interest groups, information, support, inspiration, consolation—all because the Net has created the ability to find each other and form relationships unconstrained by space and time. At first glance, it appears that the Net has introduced us to the universe of entanglements and we're all benefiting from cyberconnectivity.

But it's not that simple. We reach out to connect with others, but the medium of choice, the Net, changes the nature of how we relate. Unlike real relationships, virtual ones are highly mediated, under our control. We choose how to represent ourselves, who to talk with, when to respond, when to disappear. We can carefully control communications, and this control becomes essential as we navigate our complex, exhausting lives. A fifty-two-year-old widow reported, "After work—I want to go home, look at some photos from the grandchildren on Facebook, send some e-mails and feel in touch. I'm tired. I'm not ready for people—I mean people in person."[27]

Phone calls are quickly disappearing—they take too much time and are too open-ended. Teens feel texting is safer, less revealing; texts give them time to carefully construct their message, or not to reply at all.[28] And we overworked adults don't have time to call. Professionals report, with some guilt, that they manage their friends like clients, setting up appointments for a phone chat weeks or months in advance, no longer just picking up the phone for a casual chat. (I plead guilty to this practice.) Sherry Turkel, in her brilliant book *Alone Together: Why We Expect More from Technology and Less from Each Other,* describes how we got to this point. "The flight to e-mail begins as a 'solution' to fatigue. It ends with people having a hard time summoning themselves for a telephone call, and certainly not for 'people in person.'" She characterizes how busyness has driven us to make "a new Faustian bargain . . . if we are left alone when we make contact we can handle being together."[29]

In the relationship-rich Net, we can instantly connect with millions of people. But we are becoming less skilled and less interested in the demands of real intimacy. It's no wonder that many people report feeling disconnected and lonely.

Lonely Planet

Loneliness and isolation are nothing new to the human experience. (The loneliness of Americans has been documented since at least 1950.[30]) But now, feelings of isolation are affecting people everywhere, for different reasons. Globally, hundreds of millions of people have been displaced from their families and communities by poverty and natural disasters, forced to leave home and abandon their cultures in order to find work or to survive. For those of us with material comforts, our loneliness stems not from leaving home but from never being home. Overwhelmed by the demands of work and family, we're running in all directions, ticking off tasks, running to the next meeting or child's event. I notice how many people now describe themselves as overwhelmed and exhausted by obligations that feel increasingly meaningless.

And it is the Internet, as odd as this seems, that has been a primary contributor to the increase in loneliness. As Turkel describes it:

> As we instant-message, email, text, and Twitter, technology redraws the boundaries between intimacy and solitude. . . . Things that happen in "real-time" take too much time. Tethered to technology, we are shaken when our world "unplugged" does not satisfy. After an evening of avatar-to-avatar talk in a networked game, we feel, at one moment, in possession of a full social life and, in the next, curiously isolated, in tenuous complicity with strangers. We build a following on Facebook or MySpace and wonder to what degree our followers are friends. We recreate ourselves as online personae and give ourselves new bodies, homes, jobs, and romances. Yet, suddenly, in the half-light of virtual community, we may feel utterly alone. As we distribute ourselves, we may abandon ourselves. Sometimes people experience no sense of having communicated after hours of communication.[31]

How Has the Net Changed You?

Turkel's research has been extensive, but I believe it is easy to corroborate her findings by looking at our own behaviors. Have you changed your preferred mode of communicating with kids and colleagues? Are you now texting rather than calling? Do you prefer texting because it's faster and more efficient than phoning? Do you drop in on people or call them without an appointment or set time? If you ever make an impromptu call, do you worry you might be disturbing them? If you spend time in virtual realities, either games or simulations, do you experience what Turkel describes—suddenly lonely after hours of seeming connection?

For those of us who remember a time before exhaustion and overwhelm took over, who remember the pleasures of casual conversations and unplanned time, have we been noticing how we've changed? Have we thought about or tried rearranging our priorities so we have more time for relationships? Do we even want to go back? Do more intimate relationships seem worth the time? Or are they just another demand we'd rather avoid adding to our overscheduled lives?

The most devastating aspect of Turkel's research is her evidence that robots are on the rise as desirable alternatives to live pets, companions and even sexual partners. We are, she notes, "too exhausted to deal with each other in adversity."[32] Why choose a human when you can get a robot programmed to perform for you, preset to offer caring and companionship without any demands or problems, a no-risk relationship guaranteed to give you what you need, asking nothing in return? Already heavily marketed to seniors (such as robotic baby seals) and young children (Furbies, Zhu Zhu pet hamsters), Turkel believes that we are at "the robotic moment," ready to switch to robots not as a substitute for human interaction, but as a preferred alternative to the complexity and stickiness of human intimacy.

How ironic. Science has revealed a world of entanglements, of nonlocal intimacy, where relationships are the foundation for all that is, where relationships provide the conditions for us to realize new potentials. And now this same science is being used in technologies that offer sophisticated, preprogrammed-to-care machines to replace human relationships. A further irony is that for stressed and overwhelmed people forced to cope with the relentless pace of life created by technology, robots are an easy sell.

When Butterflies Flutter

Leaving this unfolding Orwellian scenario behind, let's return to the real world and contemplate a dramatic example of interconnectedness—the "Butterfly Effect," first revealed by a meteorologist studying chaotic weather.[33] He discovered that even the smallest of actions, such as the flap of a butterfly's wings, can move through this intensely interconnected world and escalate into big effects far from where the butterfly first fluttered. We never know the consequences of small actions as they spread through this networked world.

We see the Butterfly Effect in today's world when things "go viral," propagating and spreading with lightning speed. And I've taught for many years how change happens laterally through networks of connections that begin as small efforts. The Butterfly Effect still feels enticing, filled with hope that our small efforts can emerge as large-scale change. And perhaps butterflies will flap in our favor. But I need to point out that the majority of things that go viral on the Net are funny, bizarre, fearful, or pornographic. When something meaningful does go viral—WikiLeaks, photos that expose tragic or inhumane behaviors, investigative reports that provide evidence of great wrongdoing—it doesn't create change. It just creates temporary commotion. (There are reasons for this that you'll read about in the next part, "Lost.") Meanwhile, the Net—the seemingly great connector—continues to provide infinite opportunities for personal preferences and perversions to spin out of control.

Can We Do No Harm?

I want to end this exploration of entanglement with a very personal question. In this entangled world, is it possible to do no harm? Many people aspire to do no harm, including physicians taking the Hippocratic oath and those taking traditional Buddhist vows. This is a vow I also have taken and I've spent many hours contemplating this question: can I live my life so as not to cause pain and suffering in others? I've come to the disturbing and sad conclusion that it is simply impossible to live in this globalized world free from causing harm, unless you retreat to a cave and live completely disconnected from everyone—a person that Archbishop Tutu has described as "a subhuman." We are intimately interconnected. As recurring corporate scandals about working conditions in China, Africa, or Southeast Asia always reveal, our lives of material comfort and cheap goods are paid for by workers, too many as slaves, in sweat shops and factories. And our appetites for fresh fruit any season, good coffee and chocolate are satisfied by farmers and workers far from us suffering from poverty and hunger.

But even when we know this, what can we do? In this addictive web of consumers and cheap products, in a global economy propelled by grasping and greed, what can we do? We can protest. We can boycott. We can learn the origin of what we buy and consciously choose who to buy from. We can spend less. And these are all important, mindful moral actions.

But they won't stop consumerism as a global imperative, they won't disenfranchise the robber barons, they won't substantially change the working conditions of millions upon millions of people. We do need to take responsibility for how our actions impact others. We do need to stay conscious of the price of our choices and lifestyles. But I no longer aspire to do no harm. I have only one shred of hope in this endlessly entangled world, based on a practice I've been taught. In this practice, we consciously notice a good moment, a plate filled with food or a warm, safe bed. We take notice, express our gratitude, and then we offer this goodness to others who are in need of it. I do this practice many times a day now, grateful to have learned it, but always doubtful of its effects. Perhaps my conscious awareness of the blessings of my life travels through the web of interbeing and offers support and comfort to people far distant from me. This might be happening—the science says it's possible. But truthfully, even if it is, it's not enough. I know that many of the things I am grateful for in my life have created harm to others I will never meet.

In the next section, "Lost," I develop three maps of how we ended up in this mess of a brave new world, lost and separated from one another and from life's great creativity and generosity.

PART III

LOST

Opening to the world as it is

8

ARE WE LOST?

Are we lost?
If we were, how would we know?
When people are lost in the wilderness, they
move through predictable stages. The first
reaction is to deny they are lost.

They know where they are, they just can't find a familiar sign. They convince themselves that everything's okay. They still know where they are going; the maps are still correct. But gradually, confronted with a growing number of strange and unfamiliar sights, anxiety seeps in. They speed up their activities, fueled by a sense of urgency, needing to verify as quickly as possible that they are not lost. Those lost on a mountain walk faster; those lost in a failing project work faster and harder. Yet in spite of these urgent actions, doubt and uncertainty creep in. People become angry and impatient, pushing aside any information that doesn't confirm their map. They're desperate to find any scrap of information that proves they know where they are. They reject all other information, even that which would help them get unlost.

There comes a point when people are overcome by fear and panic—they can no longer deny that they're lost. Stressed and scared, their brains stop working. They can't think straight, so every action they take is senseless, only creating more exhaustion. Confused and panicked, people search frantically for any little sign that's familiar, any small shred of evidence that makes them feel unlost, that signals their maps are still correct. But they *are* lost, so this strategy fails and they continue to deteriorate.

Do you recognize any of these behaviors in yourself? Have you observed these behaviors in your colleagues at work? Do they describe what's going on in society? Are we lost?

We're Not Lost, We're Right Here

People lost in the wilderness, whose immediate survival is at stake, have only one option left at this point. They must accept their situation: they are truly lost. As Laurence Gonzales, author of *Extreme Survival*, clearly states, "Like it or not, you must make a new mental map of where you are or you will die. To survive, you must find yourself. Then it won't matter where you are. . . . Not being lost is not a matter of getting back to where you started from; it is a decision not to be lost wherever you happen to find yourself. It's simply saying, 'I'm not lost, I'm right here.'"[34]

When I first read Gonzales, I felt he was perfectly describing the behaviors common in our lives and organizations these days. How many of us are exhausted and overwhelmed? How many of us think that solutions can be found by working harder, faster, with more urgency? How many of us experience a sense of dread or foreboding as we realize that things are not working out as planned?

What if we were to acknowledge that we are lost, that our familiar practices and maps no longer give us the information we need to find our way through? Being lost is frightening only until we admit that we are lost. Once we stop denying our situation, our fear dissipates. Our thinking becomes clear again and we can recognize the truth of our situation. It becomes possible to settle down, quiet our minds, look around, and discover that there is more than enough information available to create a new map that accurately describes where we are, a map that can help us find our way.

The Dark Details of Where We Are
So where are we? How to describe this world that confounds our attempts to change it, that frustrates, exhausts, and imperils us? What are its features, its characteristics?

This brave new world feels like it materialized suddenly, out of nowhere, but it came from somewhere. It emerged as the result of many different values, decisions and influences interacting, intensifying, strengthening, and changing as they fed off one another. What's emerged is a powerful culture, with new and different characteristics that could not have been predicted.

Here is how I would describe our present world. I offer these statements so that we might see where we are, clearly and honestly. Even as I contemplate writing them, they are simultaneously obvious and depressing. This is a familiar experience for me—moments of clarity accompanied by feelings of overwhelming grief. These contrasting emotions always seem to come together, like hope and fear. But over many years now, I've learned to sit quietly with both. Grief, if allowed to just be there, can give way to clarity. If I don't infuse my despair with drama, if I refrain from getting caught up in outrage and righteous anger, if I can just acknowledge how terrible and overwhelmed I feel, then grief will dissipate. Once grief passes through me, clarity remains, and with that I find the strength to keep going. In the end, it is clear seeing that illuminates the path of right action and right work.

Our Present World

It is a world of intensifying emotions and positions moving to extremes, where anger has become rage, opponents have become enemies, dislike has become hatred, sorrow has become despair.

It is a world closing shut, where individuals, groups, ethnicities, and governments fortify their positions behind impermeable boundaries.

It is a world where critical thinking scarcely exists, where there is no distinction between facts and opinions.

It is a world that discredits science as mere opinion, yet still wants science to give us health, long life, security, and a way out of our problems.

It is a world where information no longer makes a difference, where we hear only what we want to hear, always confirmed never contradicted.

It is a world desperate for certainty and safety, choosing coercion and violence as the means to achieve this.

It is a world solving its crises by brinksmanship and last-minute deals, no matter how important or disastrous the consequences may be.

It is the Tower of Babel, everybody shouting and nobody listening.

It is a world growing more meaningless as lives are taken over by values of consumption, greed, and self-interest.

It is a world of people who had been effective and constructive now feeling powerless and exhausted.

It is a world whose growth, garbage and disregard will not be tolerated by the planet much longer.

I imagine that you might be reacting to these statements in one of two ways. You may be feeling confirmed for the work you're engaged in, because it addresses one or more of these trends. You may be teaching nonviolence to children, listening skills to adults, participative processes to communities, critical thinking skills to teams, high-engagement strategies to leaders. You may be actively working for social justice, the environment, worker rights, immigration reform, democracy, health equity, food justice, healthy communities. Most of my friends and close colleagues are engaged in one or more of these causes, as I have been also. I hope in these pages you will find support to keep going with your work, but to hold it differently, freed from urgency and ambition.

Or perhaps, after reading this all-negative list, you are already composing an email to me of all the positive things also going on in this world. Or describing the positive outcomes you are getting from your work, how you *are* making a difference. If you are writing that email, please recall that it is not my intent to support your hope or optimism, but your warriorship. As warriors, we need to recognize that, try as hard as we might, we are lost in a world that requires new maps. To draw new maps, we must first see this world in all its life-destroying detail and not grasp, as lost people always do, for small shreds of evidence that the old maps still work. Only as we open ourselves to the world as it is, open to the enormous tragedy of this time, will we find the skillful means and the gentleness, decency and bravery to serve this world. I have had to learn the truth of this process many times over, and now I trust it completely. I know it is the only way to discover how we get unlost, how we find the strength and confidence to do meaningful work in a terrible time.

I encourage you to sit with this list for a while and, if need be, let it lead you through the stages of denial, hopelessness, and grief until you arrive at the quiet place of accepting what is. We're not lost: we're right here. This is how we discover the path of clear seeing, sanity, and how we go forward with our work joyfully, wholeheartedly.

Three Maps for Becoming Unlost
I've been trained to see the world as a series of complex interactions, to look for multiple causes and conditions rather than just one, to be curious about what's resulted from the process of interconnecting rather than the study of isolated parts. In my own practice, more and more I find myself drawing these system's maps to maintain my own sanity. I need to understand how policies, leaders, and groups seem intent, as I heard a Chilean poet say, "on undoing the future."

The next three chapters contain systems maps of how destructive behaviors and trends developed, not on their own or in isolation, but because they interacted within an interconnected system.

9

ALL-CONSUMING SELVES

I want to understand how this culture of narcissism, polarization, and paranoia came to be; and how we became so fearful of one another, separating into categories and ethnicities just when we need to support and console one another and work together as strong communities.

So I'm undertaking to draw a map of the primary influences and dynamics that interacted to emerge as this fear-based culture. I believe this map will interest you if you've been working on nonviolence, civility, democracy, the media, consumerism, corporate power, environmentalism, community building. As you'll see here, I found them to be all interconnected, feeding on one another in complex ways, acting at different times both as cause and effect.

The first challenge in developing a system's map is to draw a boundary, just as new life forms do as their first act. This is essential in mapping a system because, without delineation, we would have to include the entire universe. Any one thing comes from everything else. As the American naturalist John Muir said: "When we try to pick out anything by itself, we find it hitched to everything else in the Universe."[35]

This map focuses on the individual self. I could go back to the Greeks, 2,300 years ago, because, among their many contributions to Western civilization, they glorified the individual. But here I draw the boundary much nearer and begin with the advent of global markets, when production, trade, and marketing went worldwide, the age of brands and logos that started its rise to dominance in the 1980s. As global consumers were aggressively pursued, life's fundamental organizing dynamic—self making—became the driving force. I don't believe that marketeers were conscious of how compelling this dynamic would be, but certainly they exploited it to the max once its power became evident.

A World of Hungry Ghosts
A global culture of consumers emerged from incessant, obsessive attention to each individual's choice of identity. What's your style? What's your taste? Create any identity you want, in real time and, even more fun, virtually. Conscious self making became the norm—you can be anything you want to be and the world will know who you are by what you wear, how you smell, what you drive, and what you eat. This consumer culture of manufactured selves has left behind more than half of Earth's seven billion people and conscripted millions of poor people to terrible working conditions to produce what we affluent consume. Yet even in poor and remote communities, the seduction of self-creation is visible as young people leave home to find their freedom. Lured by materialism, they purchase fast cars rather than homes, flashy clothes rather than healthy foods, temporary highs rather than long-term skills.

This consumption is how economies keep going, most notably in the United States where 65 percent of the economy is from consumer spending. But this need to create consumers is now global. A new mall, even in poor cities, is regarded as a sign of progress. In poor communities in the Global South, I have seen large billboards displaying pictures of Western lifestyles to sell credit cards or cigarettes. Worldwide, these ads get flashier and more insistent from necessity—if people refuse to consume, the world economy collapses. The machinery of self making must continue to bombard us with images of people living lives we think we want, creating endless needs, deliberately cultivating an insatiable world. In Buddhism, there is a class of beings known as "hungry ghosts." These beings are condemned to a life where they can never be satisfied; they're depicted with long thin necks and huge bloated bellies. Not only do their necks restrict how much they can consume, but whatever they manage to eat burns like fire and causes unbearable pain. They can never be satiated. It seems to me that our global consumer culture cultivates hungry ghosts as the means to survive.

Do You Like Me?

The dynamic of consumers defining themselves by personal tastes and preferences was already well in motion when the next giant influence appeared on the scene—the Internet and social networking. Almost overnight it became easy to describe who you were, what you were doing, how you were feeling, moment by moment in a never-ending stream of brief reports. Popularity became the primary driver, incredibly easy to track: how many friends, how many followers, how many re-tweets. But more important, the Net created a new arena for instant judgments. Thumbs up, thumbs down. Do you like or dislike this article, this review, this item? (Recently, as I was purchasing bedding on line, I was encouraged to "be the first of your friends to like this item." Apparently being an early adopter will make me more popular, although I still can't figure out why it matters to my friends for me to be first in liking a bed sheet.) Nearly every site I go to or store I walk into (even my dentist's office) now want my first action to be "Like us on Facebook." We're asked to give our opinion on everything (but only in thumb symbology). We're also told how many others liked this article, this photo, this quote, whatever you just pulled up. (When I pulled up Yeats's seminal phrase, "things fall apart, the centre cannot hold," I learned that 106 people liked this quote.)

This rampant reliance on popularity also now propels search engines. Google delivers information to individuals based on what they liked in the past; what interested you before is what you get now. Popularity even has dramatically altered academic research, where you would think the quality of the content would be primary, but it is not. Popularity rather than quality has limited the number of sources that academics use, narrowing rather than expanding how they do research. It was thought that knowledge would be advanced by making millions of articles available online, but the effect has been quite the opposite. Sociologist James Evan reviewed citations in more than thirty-four million articles published in academic journals and noted how the number of different citations declined after the advent of search engines. These information-filtering tools, he observed, "serve as amplifiers of popularity, quickly establishing and then continually reinforcing a consensus about what information is important and what isn't."[36]

Since its beginning, Google has taken a populist approach to evaluating websites, giving prominence to those receiving the most number of links and hits. The assumption was that popular sites would have the best information, never a solid assumption to begin with. But now, even popularity has been demoted by what is newest. In 2009, Google gave users the option to have their requests sorted by newness—information most recently posted. Google's founder, Larry Page, has stated that Google won't be satisfied until it can index the Web every second to allow real-time searches.[37] People who want fame, Google-style, know to post frequently on their website, some even updating content several times a day. This substitution of immediacy for quality is, of course, the premise of Twitter and Facebook. The only information that is important is what is happening right now, posted in a way to make you attractive to friends, followers, colleagues and even researchers.

Popularity also commands space on news sites—every online news service informs you of the most popular articles of the day, week, or month. I find this convenient, as most presorting is, but I shudder to think that we're only reading the articles that others, strangers whom we don't know, decided to read. But in our sped-up lives, popularity seems to be how we discriminate about where to put our precious time. No wonder we're beginning to act like lemmings.

In 2011, popularity contests attained a new level of status. CNN introduced a new feature—you got to choose which news story you wanted to watch. Viewers were given very brief descriptions of three news stories (all of which, by the way, were important) and then asked to vote on them. News morphed from information about other people that we need to know to a popularity contest of what I choose to know.

Opinions Strengthen, Paranoia Increases
This world of thumbs going up or down, the nonstop critiquing of everything, has resulted in a culture of instant, careless, meaningless judgment. If it was only individuals, it might be annoying but nothing more serious. But it exacerbates another trend that also began several years ago, that of losing the distinction between opinion and fact. Now,

we only listen to commentators whose opinions match our own, talk to people who think like us, chat online with those of same interests. Even if we'd like to stay open and curious, we're caught in a self-sealing dynamic. We don't have time or energy to engage; it's easier to just stick with those who confirm our opinions. The boundaries between us and them get stronger, and we settle in to the comfort of being only with like-minded people. We become intellectually lazy, group thinkers. From here, it's just one step to becoming more righteous about our position, more aggressive in our stance, more fearful of those who are different. This is the road leading to fundamentalism—rigid views that will not be changed, only defended. And most of us are on it.

So here we have a culture of people who have been powerfully manipulated into believing they're defined by their tastes and preferences. Highly individualized identities are given unlimited, ever-present opportunities to give their opinion. Identities become rigidly defined on the basis of these judgments: You are not like me. We don't like the same things. I don't like you. I hate you. The dividing lines become very clear. My opinions continue to be strengthened by the media and commentators I listen to; they reinforce my opinions and tell me to keep thinking this way, that I'm right and everyone else is either an idiot or dangerous. I soon forget, if I ever knew, that there's any other way to think about things. My judgments get strengthened every time I comment, vote, blog, post, listen to commentators. With every thumbs up or down, I feel more confirmed in my tastes. No one's challenging me; they just want to know what I like. My opinion is all that matters.

A culture of opinions moves in one direction, toward intensified fear and paranoia. Emotions can only intensify as positions solidify. What we disliked we now hate. People who disagreed with us now become enemies. Opposition now becomes evil incarnate. Anger becomes violent rage and attack. This descent into dark, violent emotions is predictable. Whenever people feel threatened at the level of identity, they draw a defensive boundary around themselves. They close down, wanting to protect themselves from those they think are out to destroy them. If they cracked open that boundary even for a moment by letting in a different opinion, they'd be endangering themselves.

Fear of Conversations
I've encountered opposition in bringing together diverse people in conversations in a number of places where I've worked, especially when inviting people to join a community conversation or to talk about an important issue from multiple perspectives. At first I couldn't understand why my well-intended invitation was interpreted as a threat rather than an opportunity. Over time, I came to understand that, to them, my invitation would be a crack in their defenses, a small opening that might end up destroying their identity. And I realized they were right.

When you have a rigid identity, you can't let other people's perspectives in. Conversing with them might cause you to change your mind. Even if it's just a little change, that first one might lead to the unraveling of many other beliefs. If that happened, you could no longer identify with your culture or faith—you would no longer belong. What had appeared inviting to me was accurately perceived by them as life-threatening. People feel compelled to stay with their own kind; it's too big a risk to talk with others across the borderlines. This is the price of belonging.

There's also another price that is predictable and dangerous, common throughout history. When individuals join a group, they have to accept views more extreme than those they held as individuals. We become "good soldiers," doing things we would never dream of doing had we not joined. A culture can emerge, such as one did at Jonestown, where nine hundred people "drank the Kool-Aid" when told to do so. This phrase has entered our lexicon—I hear it all the time now and I'm deeply disturbed by its current popularity. People use it to describe actions they perform for their organization that they don't support but feel compelled to go along with. Every time I hear people describe their actions in this way, I wonder if they're truly content with the role of good soldier, whether they've released themselves from independent moral judgments about what's right and wrong.

The Disrepute of Scientific Thinking

As polarizing and extreme as our opinionated culture has become, there's another consequence that has grave implications for our very survival. Science has been reduced to mere opinion, losing the distinction between fact and opinion, forgetting that there is evidence derived from careful experimentation that can be replicated in order to confirm its validity. Scientific evidence has become a problem to ignore rather than the source of solving problems. It has been demeaned and demoted to just another voice in the discussion of issues that affect our very survival, from individual health to global climate change.

Policy and political issues get decided using political biases and ideologies rather than well-established evidence. Decision makers struggle to compromise among warring opinions, treating all opinions as equal, rather than consulting evidence and facts. (It's ironic how many leaders say they want "evidence-based decision making" but, as one school administrator said, it's more accurate to describe it as "decision-based evidence making.")

Throughout history, scientists have never had an easy time when they present evidence that the rulers or the church don't want to hear. Any scientifically derived worldview, if it threatens the beliefs by which a society functions, by which rulers exert control, is labeled as heresy and the scientists are punished. Galileo was imprisoned by the Inquisition, Darwin resisted publishing his work for forty years, and today many scientists (many whose work I've cited in this book) lose their positions or funding, live with ridicule or invisibility, and may die before their work is accepted.

As in the past, science is dismissed today because it contradicts the religious views of those in power. Nowhere is this more evident than in the titanic issue of our time, global climate change. Even though the evidence confronts us daily and is experienced directly by people— more frequent natural disasters, hundred-year storms every few years, erratic weather patterns, extremes in heat and cold, glaciers melting, loss of species—politicians turn on scientists rather than deal with the evidence. We should be thinking and planning for a future of increased droughts, floods, and population demands; instead, scientists are pilloried as data manipulating, brainwashing, Godless alarmists just in it for the money.[38]

In our opinion-centric, self-manufacturing, extremist culture, it's not difficult to convince unthinking people that science is just another opinion and a highly biased one at that. We don't even notice that science, essential to solving our problems and creating a sustainable future, has disappeared from the political landscape. Candidates running for office avoid science as too controversial, too threatening to bring into a campaign. In the 2008 presidential election, the five major candidates were interviewed in 171 interviews and asked a total of nearly 3,000 questions. Of those questions, only six were about climate change (and three others were about UFOs).[39]

Shawn Otto describes this as a populist retreat from reason, a dumbing down for ideological reasons. "Science provides us with increasingly clear pictures of how to solve our great challenges, but policy makers are increasingly unwilling to pursue many of the remedies science presents. Instead, they take one of two routes: Deny the science, or pretend the problems don't exist."[40]

There's a comment I must add here. I meet so many good smart people who do know we're in trouble, who know that the planet is undergoing severe stress and change, who pride themselves on being well-informed. But after a conversation in which we've shared our understanding and despair, they brighten up and say things like, "I still have faith in human ingenuity. We're smart enough to solve these problems and invent solutions to these terrible messes."

I always feel obliged to point out that scientists and entrepreneurs *already* have created many solutions, but there doesn't seem to be much interest in using these products of human ingenuity. Solutions already are being tested by individuals and communities worldwide, some with support of their governments, many doing it as self-organized initiatives. But in this culture of opinions, ideologues and faith-based evidence making, in the halls of power where decisions are made and policies are created, we might as well ask leaders what they're doing about UFOs as about the future of the planet. There is no interest in human ingenuity, even though it is abundantly available. Rational thought does not characterize this time, extremism does. This is a culture, as poet Gary Snyder wrote many years ago, of "everything going up, up, as we all go down."[41]

How We Got Here

Could we have foreseen what's emerged, this consumption-driven, opinion-centric, paranoid culture spiraling into disaster? As I've traced its emergence here, I noted how the irresistible forces of self making, consumerism and the Internet interacted and fed on one another to begin the spiral of descent. I began with the imperative of self making, seized upon by a consumer-driven global economy. As we were cajoled, entranced, and seduced by endless opportunities to make ourselves into popular creatures, powerfully enabled by the Internet, we were negatively transformed into people of intensifying tastes and opinions. Criticism and instant judgment became the norm. Behind rigid walls of judgment and personal preferences, openness and curiosity disappeared; differences came to threaten our sense of belonging. As we became a culture of self-righteous and guarded people, did anyone care that rational thinking was disappearing, that we'd lost the distinction between facts and opinions? The clamor of opinions, voiced with ever-growing extreme rhetoric, drowned out the voice of science. Science lost its essential role of observing how the world is working and discovering solutions, not from opinions but from carefully derived evidence.

This is what's emerged, a culture of people seemingly content to defend our opinions, to deny the evidence, to ignore solutions, playing out a fate that, at its end, we most likely will rate with a thumbs down.

How would you rate this essay?

DISTRACTED
BEYOND RECALL

For years I assumed that the Titanic tragedy was a result of human arrogance, a belief in the indestructibility of the newest, largest, fastest, fanciest ship of all time.

But, in fact, the Titanic went down because of distraction. It was sailing in iceberg-filled waters, and other ships had been warning them for many days prior. The captain changed course, but only slightly, and did nothing about speed. On the night of its sinking, two ships sent warnings of icebergs, but the radio operator never passed them on. When he received a call from a ship nearby surrounded by ice, less than an hour before the collision, he responded, "Shut up, shut up, I'm busy." By the time lookouts spotted the iceberg ahead, it was too late to slow down the Titanic's nearly full-speed momentum.[42]

The *Titanic* as a metaphor for our time, while overused, is frighteningly accurate. Distracted people don't notice they are in danger. Ignorant of their vulnerability, they discount warnings or evidence that they are about to perish. My favorite quote from Rumi, the thirteenth-century Sufi mystic and poet, is "Sit down and be quiet. You are drunk and this is the edge of the roof."

How Distracted Are We?

We read reports of fatal train accidents caused by the locomotive engineer texting, of commercial flights crashing because pilots were chatting with each other; we know there are many more pedestrians and drivers killed from being on the phone or texting. And we may be aware of studies that prove people are being killed or endangered because of distracted behaviors by professionals such as doctors, bus drivers, soldiers. Such studies and reports are plentiful these days as the evidence grows that distracted people cause harm to themselves and to others.

However, we need look no further than ourselves to observe distraction. How long can you focus on any activity these days? How many pages can you read before wandering off? How often do you check email? How many other things are you doing on a conference call? How do you feel if you lose your cell phone? Have you stopped writing emails that have multiple requests because you've learned you only get a reply to the first one? Do you still take time for open-ended conversations with friends, colleagues or your children? Do you remember a time when you didn't feel you had to respond instantly to multiple demands, when your life felt more spacious, slower, when you could concentrate on a book or a problem for hours, going deeply into thought?

I vividly remember a conversation I had with my office staff the first year of fax machines. I was off-site with a client for a few days and had called into my office on a pay phone (yes, it was that long ago). My secretary offered to fax me some materials that had just come in by mail (I told you it was long ago). I remember telling her not to fax them to me because I didn't want to get distracted from the work I was doing with the client I was with—I wanted to stay present for them. Although this whole incident feels romantically implausible to me now, remembering it is a gift, a small light shining on how it used to be. It allows me to note where I am now with historical accuracy.

An Ecosystem of Interruption Technologies

T. S. Eliot wrote, "We are distracted from distraction by distraction."[43] Written in the 1930s, I can't imagine a better description of our present day. How did we get here, these lives of incessant connection but total distraction, where even if we recognize that we're hamsters on a treadmill, we can't envision any way to get out of this cage? We may not like how we're changing—if we're old enough to remember a pre-distracted era—but there is no way out as long as this world provides ever faster, more enticing means to stay connected.

Our lives, relationships and politics are being shaped, predictably and inevitably, by "an ecosystem of interruption technologies," the Internet.[44] Throughout history, technology interacts with its users in predictable ways; as we make use of it, it changes our behaviors, thinking processes, social norms and, now we know, physical brain structure. What is hard to accept is that the tools we create end up controlling us, a choiceless devolution that can only be avoided by the "Amish solution," refusing to use any technology.

I learned of the devouring, deterministic march of technology in reading the work of French philosopher, educator and political activist, Jacques Ellul in my master's program in the early 1970s. (A time when I had no difficulty reading complex books with great concentration.) Ellul's insights into history as technologically determined were developed from his active, passionate involvement with European history through both World Wars, the Spanish

Revolution, and everything else that transpired until his death in 1994. As described in Wikipedia (yes, I looked him up), he was many things: "French philosopher, law professor, sociologist, lay theologian and Christian anarchist."[45] You may not have heard of him, but it was Ellul who gave us the now-trusted concept "Think globally, act locally." I tell you all this because his perspectives and wisdom were gleaned from active engagement with the history of his time, from his unceasing curiosity and need to discern clearly what history and his experiences were teaching, using multiple lenses. (I'm not Ellul, but this is what I'm trying to do here.)

Here is the harsh clarity Ellul offers us: Once a technology enters a culture, it takes over. It feeds on itself, assisted by our eager adoption of the technology and our demands for more of it. Social structures—values, behaviors, politics—can't help but organize around technology's values; the predictable result is the loss of existing cultural values and traditions and the emergence of a new culture. Gutenberg's printing press, because it put information into the hands of everyday people, is credited with enabling the rise of individualism, literacy, complex language, private contemplation, the literary tradition and the advent of Protestantism. By 1500, just fifty years after its invention, more than twelve million books were in print in Europe. (Check it out—Google it.)

How Distracted Are You?

Many of us are eager to reject this deterministic description of human disempowerment; my professor at NYU labeled my master's thesis on Ellul "depressing." But again, we can validate how technology transforms culture by looking at what's become accepted behavior in the past few years. Do you remember when answering machines were considered rude, when people talking out loud on a street were labeled crazy, when intense, emotional conversations were held in subdued voices in private places? Do you remember having time to think with colleagues and family to work out problems, rather than just shooting off rapid-fire texts? Do you remember when you used to walk into a colleague's office to ask a question rather than fire off an email? Do you recall when you enjoyed taking time for conversation rather than just rushing to get the information you need right now? How many times have you been distracted as you've read this chapter?

If you've noted any changes in your behaviors, this is evidence of how the Internet has reshaped our culture. We might still value curiosity, exploration, contemplation, privacy, conversation, teamwork, but these are not the values visible in our day-to-day behaviors. The contradiction between what we might value and our behavior doesn't mean we're hypocrites or inauthentic; it simply shows that technology has taken over, as it always does.

Efficiency Trumps Every Other Value
The mother of all values for machines is efficiency. Machines make it possible to mass produce, mass compute, mass assemble, mass communicate, mass supervise. The nation-state as a means to exert control over large numbers of people, allegedly replacing culture and ethnicity with rationality, arose simultaneously with the Industrial Revolution.[46] That began the relentless drive for machine-like efficiency, culminating today in our current management craziness that believes anything more efficient is, of course, also more effective.

Technology has also collapsed time. Faster has become better. Products that guarantee quick results sell more than those that require discipline and patience: the twenty-one-day weight-loss program, the eight-day fitness program. Managers cannibalize successful training programs that took three days (because they involved learning and reflection) and insist they be done in three hours. As much as I'm aware of this insanity, I see it in my own behavior: I feel better when I cram more things into a day and, at the day's end, can tick off every item on my to-do list. It's a brief moment of feeling proud of my efficiency even as I know that it says nothing about how effective I've been or how meaningful the day was.

Right now, if you haven't been distracted (I just paused to send a few texts and check my email), you may be composing yet another email to me describing all the many wonderful benefits of the Internet, that it's a good technology because it makes you not only more efficient but also more effective. I agree with you. I rely heavily, constantly, on the Net: I couldn't do my work or write a book without search engines, e-books, email exchanges, and I couldn't stay connected to my family when I'm away traveling for work. However, we have to focus beyond the content, which is transfixing, and notice how we are being affected by *the process* of text, post, connect, search, scan. We are being changed in fundamental ways, losing essential human capacities. Marshall McLuhan (another profound influence on me) wrote that the content of a medium is just "the juicy piece of meat carried by the burglar to distract the watchdog of the mind."[47]

Here's my map of where distraction has led us. Again, please remember that my intention is not to describe what's happening so that we might get actively engaged in changing it. My intent is to summon us to do our work from a different perspective, beginning with the acceptance that we cannot change the titanic momentum of this culture.

Distracted by Distractions

I don't think either McLuhan or Ellul, as prophetic as they were, could have envisioned this time, when all forms of media and communication are online and reshaped in an environment of constant social exchange. The interactive nature of the Net distinguishes it from all earlier technologies; from the start, it was based on public interactions, not on private use such as with books or recordings. It fed on two powerful human needs—to be visible and to connect—at a time when we were already feeling lonely and invisible. And it gave us the means for manufacturing selves at cyberspeed. This interactivity in support of self making may explain why the Net's growth has been exponential, constantly exploding with new apps, programs, and capabilities. Our insatiability combined with technical brilliance creates a hyperactive circle of invention that some might call virtuous, but that I find deeply troubling.

We are given the means to be more distracted by more distractions which, as T. S. Eliot said, keep us from noticing that we're distracted. Even more than distraction, our growing reliance on, obsession for and addiction to the Net is destroying precious human capacities such as memory, concentration, pattern recognition, meaning making, and intimacy. We are becoming more restless, more impatient, more demanding, more insatiable even as we become more connected and creative. With the powerful forces of self making and relationships that have been set in motion, it can't be otherwise.

How Private Became Public and Vice Versa

Handheld devices, the electronic technology that ensures we are always connected, has ended what used to be a coveted experience, privacy. And simultaneously, it has destroyed public spaces. Nowadays, any public space is where we continue to carry out our private lives. It doesn't matter how many other people surround us, we're on the phone or computer or texting, continually keeping our private lives in full motion. Everyone's looking at a screen, totally involved with somewhere else.

Ironically, many people are distracted from where they are because they're broadcasting where they are, what they're feeling about where they are, or what they just saw to friends on Facebook. Others are oblivious to where they are, conducting business, dealing with an issue, making plans for some other time than now. Yet even as we stay intensely focused in our private worlds, we're freely making those public either through social media or through loud phone calls. I can't count the number of times I've been forced to listen to calls in airports where people are yelling at each other, swearing profusely, or negotiating a bitter divorce.

We go through our days making private experiences public. Many, especially younger people, seem to need a constant audience. We don't just hike in an inspiring land-scape; we immediately post pictures of ourselves there on Facebook. Reading on Kindle, I can convert a private moment to a public one by clicking on "Popular High-lights" to see what others found interesting. People feel they're complimenting me as a keynote speaker by telling how many tweets they sent while listening to me. Some churches encourage people to tweet during the service, exchanging spiritual insights. Some technophiles are cre-ating the means for people sitting in the same theater to exchange their reactions and opinions as they watch the play. (Shoot me now.)

We're always telling a story about ourselves, shaping the experience rather than just having it or keeping it to ourselves. We experience something just long enough to form an image or impression, then we broadcast it in a few words, using nondescriptive adjectives like *awesome, weird, sweet, cool*. The subtlety and complexity of experience disappear into a single word, into a single emotion; every experience is either good or bad, like or dislike. (I try hard to get my grandchildren to tell me in more detail why an experience was awesome. As bright as they are, it takes great prodding to get to any other descriptors, I feel like I'm making an unfair request of them.)

The continual opportunity, now almost a necessity, to narrate your life as you're living it is, of course, well nourished by life's dynamic of self making. Some might think that these constant narrations are modern-day storytelling, but they don't deserve that title. They're brief, disconnected, chronicles of instant, moment-to-moment reactions without any narrative thread. We just want to make sure that our friends know where we are, and that they like us.

Whatever Happened to Thinking?
This loss of capacity to describe experiences in anything over 140 characters or in descriptive language compounds a more serious consequence of working and living with the Internet. We are rapidly losing the ability to think long and hard about anything, even those issues or topics we care about. Scanning used to feel exhilarating as we found information that could help our research or teach us something interesting that we hadn't known before— and wouldn't have discovered without the Net. But now

scanning has become the only thing we do. As a museum curator commented, "The Internet has made disruption and montage the operative bases of everyday experience."[48] Hyperlinks, which seemed to offer the possibility of going deeper into a subject, of drawing our own conclusions by consulting many sources, instead have been proven to reduce learning. We don't concentrate—we flit, moving restlessly from one link to another. It may seem like we're in the process of discovery, but many studies now show that multimedia environments—with links, photos, videos, bottom text crawls—don't encourage learning and retention. So much information overloads our circuits. An overtaxed brain can't concentrate and, once in that state, finds any distraction more distracting. We lose all ability to sort or figure out what's important, which then only increases our stress.[49] I've certainly experienced this many times—I start a search, click on several links, then suddenly realize I'm feeling overwhelmed and unsettled, forgetting where I was in my thought process or why I started this search anyway, unable to remember what I just read or where to go back to find something I thought would be useful. Other research describes that students are more likely to say they didn't learn anything, or that it was meaningless material if presented in a multimedia format.[50]

Nicolas Carr, in his compelling book *The Shallows: What the Internet Is Doing to Our Brains,* describes us as minds consumed by the medium. "The Net seizes our attention only to scatter it. We focus intensively on the medium itself on the flickering screen, [to the exclusion of what's going on around us,] but we're distracted by the medium's rapid-fire delivery of competing messages and stimuli."[51] He quotes Seneca, the Roman philosopher from two thousand years ago: "To be everywhere is to be nowhere."[52]

The Loss of Collective Vision

The Net, by design, gives individuals the capacity to fragment information and use it however they choose. Because I work with artists whenever I can, I'm noticing what's happening to artistic vision because of the Net. It's common practice to take apart movies, music albums, literary works, TV shows and reconstruct these fragments into personal movie channels, playlists, favorite quotes, and so on. This is the Net's blessing, how it's unleashed infinite personal creativity. But our ability to pick and choose among artistic works comes at a price for artists and the role they play in society. Historically, artists have served their cultures by offering alternate, often uncomfortable or strange ways of seeing. I note that artists often act as prophets—they see the future first. When we cannibalize an artistic work, we aren't interested in seeing life from the artist's perspective or contemplating his or her vision; instead, we extract only those bits and pieces that confirm our own feelings.

And this is just one consequence of the Net's enticements. Today, there are hundreds of millions of personal filters operating at cyberspeed, using others' expressions out of context, selecting what parts they like, constructing selves for public viewing. What's being created is millions of individual identities, brilliantly displayed. What's being lost is a sense of collective identity, of shared meaning that transcends the individual and brings coherence to a culture. We've lost the capacity and will to enter into each other's perceptions, to be curious to see the world from another point of view.

Our insatiable appetites for self-creation and self-expression have transformed us into twenty-first-century hunter-gatherers. We've become addicted to what else we might find, where the next click might lead us, so we incessantly keep hunting. Sadly, we resemble our ancient forebears in other ways—we've abandoned the thinking skills we humans developed over many centuries of evolution: abstract thinking, nuanced language, envisioning, moral reasoning, the scientific method. Overwhelmed by inputs, caught in our self-sealing cycles, we devolve. We devolve into rigid opinions that drive us apart, into self-manufactured people lonely for acceptance, into hungry ghosts grasping for the next new thing to satisfy them.

I chose the word *devolve* very carefully.

The End of Rational Thinking
The most dire consequence of this instant-access-information-rich world is that it's changed the very nature and role of information. In life, information is the source of all change. From all the information available in its environment, an organism is free to choose what to notice. It's also free to choose how to react to what it notices. An organism pays attention to information that will enable it to survive; it discounts all other as noise. When it does pay attention, it uses that information to preserve itself; it will change in whatever way is necessary to ensure its survival. (If you got distracted and missed it, go back to Chapter 6, "Identity: The Logic of Change.")

Gregory Bateson defined information as that which makes a difference. It has to make a difference to the individual. What seems so apparent these days is that information no longer plays this pivotal, life-changing role. No matter how reputable the science, or how in-depth and thorough the investigative reporting, no matter the photos and evidence, we sort through the information with our well-formed filters. Information doesn't change our minds; it doesn't make a difference. We use any report or evidence merely to intensify our assaults on the other's opinions. In this Tower of Babel, the only thing that has changed is that rational thinking has disappeared. We don't want our minds changed; we just want more places we can shout out our opinions.

What happens when humans aren't interested in disconfirming information, when reason plays no significant part in our decision making? History records the fate of those who forgo reason, deliberation, reflection, when they choose to fight for self-protection rather than work together for a reasonable decision. People focused on self-defense, who choose fear over reason, invite in demagogues. Leaders find it easy to convince people who no longer use their intelligence. Too many good and reasonable people have been manipulated by demagogues to support destructive and disastrous actions.

Why the World Seems So Random
When we no longer rely on reason and analysis, when we react but don't think, the world becomes chaotic, unpredictable, random. It seems as if there's no order, no predictability, only chaos, but what we fail to notice is that we're projecting our own irrational behavior onto the world. Events seem to come out of nowhere and, just as fast, recede into nowhere. Life feels ever more unpredictable and, in the face of so much uncertainty, thinking seems a waste of time. Why bother, it's all so random. We don't prepare for natural disasters; we mock leaders who take time to make decisions as "indecisive"; we refuse to read well-developed analyses; we criticize complex legislation for its page length. And in our day-to-day work lives, we ask for five-minute presentations and elevator speeches to "get" whatever the issue is. If something is complex and requires more time to understand, we're not

interested—we're too busy. Just like the radio operator on the Titanic.

The world, of course, is neither random nor chaotic. It's our human irrationality that is making it appear so. Before every natural and manmade disaster, the information is there that could have been used to prepare for or prevent a tragedy. After every disaster, I wait to see how long it takes to reveal the information that was suppressed, the voices of warning that were silenced. This is always the case. A month before the terrible mine disaster in West Virginia that killed twenty-five men in April 2010, some workers had refused to go down into the mine in the preceding month. Before the economic collapse, a few people saw the illusion for what it was (and were able to profit from the meltdown). One year before Katrina, the federal government had simulated just such a catastrophic hurricane, but officials failed to do the prep work specified in their action plans.

As we deteriorate in our precious human capacities to think, to envision, to work together, to find meaning in something beyond our selves, life seems ever more random and senseless. We have made this world into an unpredictable and terrible monster because we've refused to learn about it and work with it intelligently. And the ultimate terrible loss, what we are sacrificing, is the future. Thinking forward is an impossibility for people fearfully reacting to the present moment. Tibetan cosmology includes a class of beings who "hurl the future away from themselves," as far from their awareness as possible.[53] Seems they saw us coming.

How We Got Here
Who would have imagined that a technological achievement of such transforming proportions as the Internet

would have led to the erosion of human reason? And yet it was predictable in the history of how a new technology always transforms human cultures. The Net began as an exhilarating means to find each other across the planet. In a culture obsessed with self making, technology provided the means to spiral into the personal with increasing intensity. Once handheld communication devices appeared, we never left our private lives no matter where we were; public spaces and collectively shared experience gave way to constant narration of personal experience. And as we surfed, clicked, and linked on the Net, discovering things that interested us, we didn't notice that we were losing fundamental human capacities such as memory, meaning making, and thinking. We were paying a terrible price for instant access to everything, but we were too distracted to even notice. Information, the fundamental source of change, lost its essential role. Distracted but not informed, with no patience or time to think, the world now looms as increasingly chaotic. We lost our sense-making capacity but didn't notice that it was we who were no longer making sense. As the world appeared more and more irrational, we lost interest in the future. It was just too random.

The greatest capacity of humans, the one that distinguishes us from other species, is our consciousness. We can look forward and back. We can dream and envision. We can ask "Why?" and develop cultures and religions that answer that question. We can imagine, invent, design, and bring those ideas into reality. What is so terribly tragic about this time is to watch this astonishing human capacity disappearing. And with it, all hope to avoid the iceberg looming dead ahead.

CONTROLLING COMPLEXITY

This map has been the most difficult one for me to write and I've worried that you might find it too dark to read. So I'd like to tell you a little about this map and its origins.

The world I know best is that of large organizations and governments; I've worked in many countries and at all levels, from CEOs and cabinet ministers to staff and hourly workers. I have direct and frequent experience with what I've written here; daily these dynamics severely impact those in large bureaucracies with whom I work.

As this map took shape, as I linked together so many destructive dynamics, it was impossible not to succumb to anger and despair. I have vowed not to add to the aggression and fear of this time, but I struggled to avoid doing this here. This analysis makes clear (at least to me) how much harm is being done to the good work of good people, how people with legislative authority exert that power in destructive and abusive ways, and how the future is being cast aside for private profit. We have to feel angry and outraged—these are legitimate and necessary reactions. But I also know that we can't use these to motivate us, that we need to pause long enough for them to abate so that they open the way to clarity and insight.

This map traces how the pattern of destructive and corrupting power took hold. It explains the out-of-control growth of bureaucracy and why that will not cease as leaders continue to lose control of the overly complex organizations they created in their arrogance. It also describes how we lost the capacity to deal intelligently with complex problems after extreme, oppositional politics took over. And lastly, this map explains why the powerful, no matter how corrupt or destructive, will remain in power, using their power for personal gain.

Order Without Control
As I witness the increasing anguish of my friends and colleagues—all smart and dedicated people—it feels like we are in a dark tunnel, with no light yet visible at the end. However, as I once heard a manager say, "I can't see the light but I think I've identified the tunnel." This darkening tunnel is one of increasingly trivialized, sometimes mean-spirited demands and scrutiny from desperate leaders. They are desperate to control organizations that are not only too big to fail, but also too big to lead. Uncertainty terrifies all of us but, for leaders, it's not in their job description; all leaders, even progressive ones, gain legitimacy by appearing to be in control. However, as they reach for control, leaders are choosing precisely the wrong strategies and tools. They are trying to control complex systems by external imposition. Complex systems are capable of self-regulation, of ordering themselves, but only from internal coherence to agreed-on values.

Before I map how we got into this cycle of escalating bureaucracy that makes us impotent in the face of life's uncertainty and complexity, let's relax for a moment and recall where we are in this universe filled with complex systems that find order for free, that create rather than destroy life.

Nature's complex systems achieve order without control, order that displays itself in patterns of great beauty. The intricate, infinite patterns of fractals and the rhythmic beauty of strange attractors mesmerize with their revelations of life's deep harmony.[54] These exquisite patterns are self-organization made visible—diverse and plentiful parts interacted and interpenetrated to create a well-ordered system.

Systems begin to form in life as individuals recognize that they have neighbors who they must get along with to survive. Individuals develop relationships, adapting their needs and changing their behaviors so that life works for them and their neighbors. In organizing their behaviors, every individual uses the same rules or principles. In an ecosystem, different species self-organize according to natural laws; we humans self-organize around shared values, clear agreements, norms, culture. This is a process of bounded freedom or semiautonomy: individuals are free to make choices within the boundary set by shared agreements. Over time, a system emerges that serves both individuals and the whole. This well-ordered system arises from powerful cohering forces—every participant makes choices and regulates its behavior using the same rules or values. The beautiful order of complexity arises from deep within the system, from internal coherence, not external control.[55]

Although nature's deeply patterned order has been known by humans for thousands of years, displayed in such universal symbols as the spiral, we've been able to gaze deeply into this order because of new science. Complexity science came into being with high-speed computers and new mathematical techniques, including such fields as the delightfully named "fuzzy logic." These new techniques revealed that complex systems display their order as shapes, not numbers. It is not possible to see order in graphs, data points, or snapshots; order only becomes visible as repeating patterns. These patterns are rich in information about what is going on in the system and also very useful guides to understand what will likely happen next.

Complexity Goes to Wall Street
It is no surprise that complexity science was quickly seized upon by those eager to make money. Mathematics took over Wall Street as the preeminent tool, tossing reason and common sense out the window. The 2008 financial collapse was the result of unimaginably complicated formulas and investment instruments that no one could understand constructed from information that was invalid, incomplete, misrepresented, and dangerous. Alan Greenspan, after the crash and by then retired as head of the Federal Reserve, admitted that these formulas were incomprehensible to him and the hundreds of expert economists he worked with. Investment instruments were greedily created without understanding their contents. Rating agencies then assessed them as prime investments, even though they contained about 80% high risk loans. In fact, no one knew what was in them.[56]

The very complexity of the formulas was used to *reassure* some investors that these were sound investments. As Nassim Taleb, professor of risk engineering and financial prophet, has often pointed out: "Never before in the history of man have we created so much complexity combined with so much ignorance in understanding its properties."[57] During congressional hearings after the collapse, one financial leader pleaded that they had no way to see this coming, that the meltdown was "an act of God." But God wasn't involved; it was the all-too-familiar story of a few people blinded by greed, assured of their invincibility, creating the conditions for unavoidable collapse.

All systems create themselves from self-organization, organizing around an identity. Behaviors, norms, cultures arise from this process. Normally, we try to fix bad behaviors or dysfunctional patterns at the surface level by reprogramming people's behaviors or changing bosses (which leads to a lot of wasted effort and money). To understand where behaviors come from in a complex system, we need to discern the identity. What values gave rise to these behaviors? What seem to have been the values and agreements people used as they made decisions and determined a course of action?

I believe we can explain why leaders continue to lead us on the road to nowhere by discerning their values-in-use. I would name these life-destroying values simply as greed and power. As these values manifest in actions, they are fueled by some very strong and negative beliefs about other people. Here is what I discern as their beliefs:

~ A profound distrust, even disdain, for most people
~ A belief that such people need to be controlled
~ A belief in their own inherent superiority, entitling them to take as much as they can
~ A belief that size proves superiority—bigger shows you're better

If these values are so destructive of the lives of so many, why can't we change them? Why can't we organize around values that create healthy human lives for more people? Of course, many of us have been doing just this, founding our work on robust, humane values that we spend years embedding in our work and organizations. But when we choose life-affirming values and practices, we are engaging in radical acts that go against the culture. Destructive values have taken hold and, every day, in spite of our best efforts, they are strengthened by two dynamics that keep accelerating our relentless march to the cliff. These two are command-and-control leadership, and how failing systems are rescued from collapse. Here is my understanding of why the powerful will continue to remain in power and continue to exert that power for their own, not the collective, advantage.

Too Big Not to Fail
Let's start with the belief that bigger is better, or, more accurately, "I'll show you I'm better by building bigger." Mergers and consolidations continue to create organizations too large to be led. Size is an expression of ego, not of effectiveness. (Some business texts list ego needs as a factor in corporate mergers.) The creators of these behemoths blithely assume that size doesn't matter, that organizations of any scale can be managed in the same way as always, by command and control. But size matters absolutely; it creates qualitative not just quantitative differences. You can't keep doubling a recipe and expect the same cake. A breeze is different from a hurricane; a stream is different from a flood; an entrepreneurial start-up is different from a large bureaucracy. As systems grow in size, they manifest new properties, more complexity, and more difficulties. And complex systems, no matter their size,

can never be managed well by imposed controls. Complex systems are self-regulating, which they achieve from coherence not coercion.

Morbidly obese organizations and governments are challenging leaders everywhere. How do you get them to work? What is good leadership in this environment of unprecedented volatility, where forecasting, planning, and budgeting fall victim to uncertainty and unpredictability? Of course it is critical that leaders take time to think about these new realities, but thoughtfulness hardly describes decision making these days. Instead, in an atmosphere of self-protection, anxiety, and loss of control, most leaders grasp to control and stabilize anything within their reach which is, of course, the organization. They clamp down on staff, put more policies in place, push, punish, and threaten people, people they never did trust. Because they don't trust the people they lead, their decision to rule through coercion is predictable. When you distrust people, you don't engage them in decision making, you don't share information, you don't give them an inch (because they'll take a mile). Instead, effective leadership is defined as how well you enforce the rules.

After all these years, you would think leaders would have learned that distrustful, compliance-enforcing behaviors only lead in one direction—to demotivated, demoralized, disaffected, and disappearing workers and colleagues. People's motivation and commitment degenerate in direct proportion to the amount of control and distrust in the environment. But this learning hasn't taken hold because other values are more important to most leaders: the need to be in control and to maintain one's power at all costs over people who are inferior to you.

These dynamics are in full motion: gigantic, inherently unmanageable organizations mired in internal complexity, led by people who don't trust those they lead, who scramble to maintain control of what cannot be controlled by imposing ever more coercive measures. Regulations, laws, policies, measurements proliferate to make sure that nobody gets away with anything, that no one takes advantage, that everyone is held accountable because, after all, they are the problem. It is not even ironic to note that these are the very behaviors people in power exhibit, taking advantage of the system, freely acting above the law, indifferent to the harm they are doing. They project their self-serving, destructive behaviors on to the rest of us, passing laws and regulations to stop us from doing what we are not, but they are.

Counting Ourselves into Oblivion
The global management culture's reliance on numbers compounds the unmanageability of obese bureaucracies. Nothing alive, in all its rich complexity, can be understood using only numbers. Nothing. Yet numbers give the appearance of control—they can be manipulated on spread sheets, budgets and reports to give the impression of balance and progress. Simple numbers distort and falsify reality; we focus on minutiae and become indifferent to anything else. We don't take time or have any interest in noticing patterns, dynamics and trends, things that would actually inform us about a complex system.

While complexity scientists and mathematicians have invented many statistical methods that reveal interactions, clusters and patterns, bureaucrats have used computing power to disaggregate complex human behaviors into growing lists of separate behaviors and feelings. Employee attitude surveys typically are constructed as long lists of discrete behaviors that people check off quickly and very cynically. These lists are then analyzed one factor at a time, and new programs and policies are put in place to deal one by one with each problematic factor. So much for thinking systemically about complex causes and conditions.

Dependency on simple numeric measures has numbed us down; reality appears simple and manageable again. If you want fiscal responsibility, just decrease expenses; if you want democracy, just bring in more people to vote; if you want to lose weight, just count calories. We are counting ourselves into oblivion, but we may be too exhausted and too busy to notice. If we're good at our job, we become experts at manipulating numbers to create a favorable impression so we can get refunded or reelected. We learn how to play the numbers game.

But now, even the rules of the game have changed; it is not just manipulation of numbers that matters. This game has a new ace up the sleeve of ideologues and self-serving power brokers. Anything we do can be used against us, not because we did wrong, but because someone doesn't want us around. Numbers can be changed, discarded, or ignored if those in power are out to destroy us. This reached Orwellian proportions in April 2011 when one of the U.S. Senate's most influential Republican leaders put out outrageously distorted information to attack the well-established nonprofit Planned Parenthood. When called on his deliberate lie, his office replied, "His remark was not intended to be a factual statement."[58]

The Raging River of Regulatory Demands

Wherever I go, I meet overworked, high-performing leaders and administrators struggling to keep their heads above water in a raging river of regulatory demands. The violence of this raging river is different from the past, because now some of those with lawmaking powers are using those powers to destroy the work of those they don't like or can't profit from. This is a sea change from the past, when new policies and laws were written to achieve better outcomes or to ensure productive work. Laws, policies and regulations have become a weapon against those programs and people that lawmakers want to get rid of, not because of poor performance but because of ideological differences.

I've heard this frightening scenario from many life-affirming leaders who work in large bureaucracies at very senior levels. The provost of a leading state university described how he has to deal daily with opposition from state legislators and special-interest groups: "Every day it's another psychotic event." A woman CEO described the many reasons for her exhaustion and frustration:

> *It's both the sheer volume of regulations and the viciousness behind them. We have to comply with a myriad of [sic] regulations—they come at us from all directions, local to federal. There used to be time for performance while feeding the bureaucracy, but now we're consumed by regulations and the constant monitoring and auditing of our performance. In the past, we always had more regs than we could comply with, but the consequences are different now. With competition for scarce resources, other organizations become predators, wanting to destroy those who have the money so they can grab it. So any mistake, no matter how slight, can cost you your funding*

if someone else wants it. And another terrible change—
it used to be that legislation addressed issues and prob-
lems, but now we see that legislators write legislation for
vindictive reasons; they want to get back at someone for
something. Legislation has become the means to destroy
the programs and people they dislike, no matter how
good a job they're doing. We're doing great work, and we
have lots of evidence to prove that, but how much longer
can we go on in this environment? I'm exhausted, angry,
frustrated.[59]

How did we get to this place where those in power feel
free to use their power to destroy what they dislike?
Where even decent, well-meaning legislators who support quality programs think that the best way to help is
to pass more laws? How long can good leaders and fine
programs keep going? Some are furiously treading water,
some have given up, some keep going from outrage, and
some have been dragged to the bottom by fear and stress.
Why is work such a battlefield, where good leaders have
to use their precious energy and time in fighting meaningless battles just to survive a bit longer?

Finding Meaning, but Not at Work
In a culture of overworked, stressed, demoralized and polarized workers, the relentless increase in measures, reports,
and nonsensical demands impact people emotionally,
physically, spiritually. Even if the work itself is still meaningful, the demands on those doing the work are demean-
ing and meaningless. People give up, becoming nearly
robotic, just doing what they're told because it makes no
difference anyway. We stop expecting work to be meaningful and go elsewhere to find it, to creative interests
(formerly known as hobbies), to family, volunteer service,

or online virtual realities. (Corporate training programs that focus on meaning at work are on the rise, of course.)

Online environments are particularly enticing for some. Since we can't find meaning in good teamwork, shared purpose and community, we go online to create identities, find new friends, choose more desirable lifestyles. We take our creativity into virtual realities and design purposeful lives by fleeing the real world of work and family. This is a tragic disconnect from reality, as described in earlier essays, but it bears witness to one of the great needs we humans have, to find meaning and purpose in our lives.

Too Tired to Think

We live on this beautiful planet, this indivisible whole where everything depends on everything else. As we do our work, focused on meaningless minutiae, it is increasingly hard to remember that we are participating in something "bigger than both of us." And we have more than enough to do just attending to our lists and tasks. We don't want to know that we're interconnected; this would be just one more demand on our already exhausted brains. We may feel terrible for the suffering of other people, but we have no time or brain power to think about why something has happened, what might have caused this problem or situation. Even though everything arises from multiple causes and conditions, stressed and overwhelmed people can't think. We don't want to hear about multiple causation. It is much simpler to blame one person or one cause and be done with it.

Think about what happens when something goes wrong, at home, at work, or in your community. Do you take time to think about what just happened, considering a com-plexity of causes? Or do you immediately scramble to find someone to blame or some singular reason for why this happened? Of course, you yourself are never the problem. And actually, this is true: no one person is ever the single cause of a problem.

Politicians, who should be responsible for an entire region or community, now represent single causes. Wit-ness the common scenario for decision making evident in many nations, especially those decisions and policies that affect the welfare of millions of people or a nation's economic future. Multiple causes and conditions are sel-dom brought up for consideration. There may be ample evident that decision makers should be thinking about multiple causation. They could notice that a past deci-sion focused on fixing just one problem created myriad unintended consequences, that instead of solving one problem twenty more were created. (Always, it's the unin-tended consequences that reveal our entanglements. We made a decision oblivious to how it would affect others; it's not until they get pissed at us that we realize we're connected.)

But decision makers don't seem to care that their myo-pic, self-serving behaviors are creating more problems. Instead, the political debate stays structured on single issues, simple cause and effect. Perhaps politicians can't handle complex thinking or don't think we can; perhaps they vehemently defend single issues to amass power; perhaps there's no choice in this polarized, opinion-only culture; perhaps as citizens we're too busy to pay atten-tion, or we're too disgusted by political posturing and we just turn away.

Why Problems Don't Get Solved

Of course there are multiple causes for this atrocious political decision making, but what is most important to notice is how causes vector in to create a common yet ominous pattern to public policy decisions. Here's the scenario I see in many advanced democracies these days: Politicians and leaders claim their position. There's a great deal of posturing and displaying. They roil the waters of discontent and use fear to solidify their base, inducing a horrific future if they don't win on this issue, or if the opposition gets its way. (This is the only way the future ever enters these rants.) Language grows more extreme as slander and epithets are hurled across the divide. Online misinformation, more and more of it deliberately planted to induce fear and distrust, spreads like wildfires. Slander, lies, media hysteria, citizen fear—all feed on each other until finally, because decision makers have run out of time, a last-minute deal is reached. The issues have not been resolved, only postponed to a future time when leaders will then, allegedly, use reason rather than hysteria to determine what to do. But this doesn't happen. Instead, the divisions become more extreme and politicians perfect their tactics. They use their positional power to hold hostage governments and critical legislation until they get their way.

Why the Foxes Get to Fix the Chicken Coop

There is one more dynamic that strengthens those in power, even as they wreak destruction: those who get called in to fix a system too big to fail. Many people have commented on this dynamic in the 2008 financial meltdown. Those brought into the government and given formal authority to solve the problem were the very people who had caused the problem.[60] In their extremely well-researched book, *Reckless Endangerment: How Out-sized Ambition, Greed, and Corruption Led to Economic Armageddon*, Pulitzer Prize–winning business reporter Gretchen Morgenson and Joshua Rosner write:

> *Familiar as we are with the ways of Wall Street, neither Josh nor I was surprised that the large investment firms played such a prominent role in the debacle. But we are disturbed that so many who contributed to the mess are still in positions of power or have risen to even higher ranks. And while some architects of the crisis may no longer command center stage, they remain respected members of the business or regulatory community. The failure to hold central figures accountable for their actions sets a dangerous precedent. A system where perpetrators of such a crime are allowed to slip quietly from the scene is just plain wrong.*[61]

No matter how outraged we are, this is the catch-22 of this time. To avoid further calamitous collapse, we have no option but to call in those responsible for the initial collapse, those who know the inner workings of the system. It doesn't matter that, from the very start, these systems never took us into account. It doesn't matter that they were created from values that discounted, distrusted, and ignored us. They are now the dominant powers that impact our lives. If they fail, we all go down; they truly are too big to fail. And nobody understands them or how to manipulate them back to some type of functioning except those who created them.

It shouldn't be this way. One of Nassim Taleb's principles for restoring sanity to the financial world is "People who were driving a school bus blindfolded (and crashed it) should never be given a new bus."[62] But we continue to give them the bus, and any other vehicle they want; and I believe we have no choice if we want to put off total collapse.

Every time we give back the keys to the bus, they seem to pull the system out of its near-meltdown through back-room deals. But we'd be extremely foolish to think that anything has changed, that now the system will benefit us. And even when we see what is going on, we don't have any real influence. We try to regain some power the only way we know how: by clamoring for reform and more oversight. But do we really believe that this system designed to benefit the few can be controlled through new laws and watchdogs? System insiders, now in official positions, play along with us, seemingly complying with citizen demands for increased regulation.

But who is most impacted by these new regulations? We are—they aren't. In the financial industry, increased regu-lations have made it harder for everyday people and small businesses to get mortgages and loans, while the wealth of banks and corporations has risen to historic highs in direct proportion to the amount of government funds given to them after the crash. They sit on the largest cash reserves in modern history. As Morgenson and Rosner comment, this was "the maddening aftermath—watching hundreds of billions of taxpayer dollars get funneled to rescue some of the very institutions that drove the coun-try into the ditch."[63]

What else could we expect when we give the foxes author-ity to fix the chicken coop? There's no change in their predator identity; the foxes just get more clever in feigning concern, all the while designing less obvious routes to the chickens. And also successfully affixing blame for all those dead chickens on us.

Nothing changes in life without a change in identity. If we were to put a stop to this system that is destroying the present and future, we would need to be able to change its underlying values. Most of us know they are destructive. And so do our young people. They withdraw from the scene, refusing to vote, convinced that it's all a vicious game. They go online and participate actively in creating better worlds in virtual space while the real world crashes and burns.

Could we do it differently? Could we not rely on insiders to fix problems they created? Could we instead let these systems collapse, live through the consequences, and create new institutions and governments using healthier values? Well, total systems' collapse is far from a desirable outcome, because those who would suffer most would be the innocents, us everyday people. These systems are most likely collapsing anyway, but pushing this off to the future may be making it possible for a few less people to suffer. At least I hold this as a possibility. We need to use whatever time we have to create stronger relationships and community. This is our work as warriors.

How We Got Here
This insanity, and its relentless path to self-destruction, began with the arrogance familiar in most leaders. Twentieth-century leaders built corporate empires, organizations too big to lead. Inherently unmanageable by virtue of size and complexity, inherently meaningless by virtue of work reduced to disassociated parts, these behemoths were ill

prepared for this new world of rapid change and unpre-dictability. Faced with growing uncertainty and instability, leaders didn't understand complexity for its order-seek-ing capacity achieved through self-regulation. And they didn't trust the people working for them. So they chose the familiar means of coercion and control, creating laws, regulations, policies, measurements. These bureaucratic means did not reduce the chaos; in fact, they created more unpredictability as unintended consequences bur-geoned and worker cynicism escalated. Although the chaos was self-induced, leaders still don't know what else to do except to tighten controls, putting strangleholds on performance.

People withdraw from work, even formerly satisfying work, and look for meaning elsewhere, in self-creation activities. Some seek refuge from their growing sense of fear and dread by identifying an enemy, spurred on by political rhetoric and distorted information. Other exhausted peo-ple have no time for complexity and tiredly go along as politicians reduce complex problems to simplistic cause and effect.

Those in power maintain control by fear-based emotional manipulation. Rational decision making disappears. Politi-cians use their position to get what they want, destroy what they dislike, and employ extreme measures to ensure they win. And every time we approach systems collapse, we have no choice but to rely on those in power to save the system, perpetuating the survival of systems that serve very few and profoundly disserve the many.

This is the political and social system that has emerged, organized from values of greed and power. It emerged, like all systems, from many different elements interacting; and now that it's here, it possesses new powers, new destructions. Like all emergent phenomena, it surprises us with its appearance. This is not what we intended to happen. And as clearly as we see its destructive power, we cannot change it because it is emergent.

As the suffering wrought by greed and power continues to escalate, my aspiration is that we move beyond outrage and despair to clarity, clearly seeing that we must claim a new role for ourselves.

In the next section, "Found," I explore in depth what it means to choose the path of warriors for the human spirit.

PART IV

FOUND

We may discover that gentleness, decency, and bravery are available not only to us but to all human beings.

12

A PROPHECY
OF WARRIORS

*"There comes a time when all life on Earth
is in danger. Great barbarian powers have arisen.*

Although these powers spend their wealth in preparations
to annihilate one another, they have much in common:
weapons of unfathomable destructive power, and technologies that lay waste our world. In this era, when the
future of sentient life hangs by the frailest of threads, the
Shambhala warriors appear."

The warriors have no home. They move on the terrain of
the barbarian powers. Great courage is required, both
moral and physical, for they must go into the heart of the
barbarian powers to dismantle their weapons, into the
places where the weapons are created, into the corridors
of power where decisions are made.

The Shambhala warriors are armed only with the weapons of compassion and insight. Both are necessary. Compassion gives them the energy to move forward, not to
be afraid of the pain of the world. Fueled by compassion,
warriors engage with the world, step forward and act. But
by itself compassion burns with too much passion and
exhausts us, so the second weapon is needed—insight
into the interdependence of all phenomena.

With that wisdom we see that the battle is not between "good guys" and "bad guys," because the line between good and evil runs through every human heart. And with insight into our profound interrelatedness, we discern right action, knowing that actions undertaken with pure intent have repercussions throughout the web of life, beyond what can be measured or discerned.

Together these two weapons sustain the warriors: the recognition and experience of our pain for the world and the recognition and experience of our radical interconnectedness with all life.

—Adapted from Dugu Choegyal,
as recounted by Joanna Macy[64]

13

CHOOSING FOR THE HUMAN SPIRIT

What is your experience with humans that would inspire you to choose to become a warrior for the human spirit? Are people really worth the struggle?

Chögyam Trungpa, the founder of Shambhala training, taught that dark times arise when people lose faith in one another. Absent that positive belief in others, there is no motivation to act courageously. People disappear into their private worlds, just as is happening now. If we choose to be warriors, we will find ourselves struggling day to day to be wise and compassionate as we work inside the collapsing corridors of power. We have to expect a life of constant challenge, rejection, invisibility, and loneliness. So it's important to contemplate how much faith you have in people, because this is what gives you courage and the ability to persevere. What has been your direct experience with the best qualities of the human spirit, with human goodness?

Chögyam Trungpa also taught, "Something that is worthwhile, wholesome and healthy exists in all of us."[65] Have you discovered this in your life and work? Have you discovered that we truly are, all of us, bundles of potential, capable of manifesting new talents and skills? How many times have you been surprised by someone suddenly displaying new capacities, ones you never would have expected from them? How many times have you surprised yourself? And what's been your experience with generosity and compassion? How often have you witnessed or benefited from others' compassion generously offered, when they worked hard to help you or another person without concern for themselves? Certainly we witness this after every natural disaster, strangers rushing in to assist, people helping people with no thought for their own needs or safety.

Gentleness, Decency, and Bravery Are Available

The quote that has served to structure this book provides another way to directly experience human goodness. "By opening to the world as it is, we may find that gentleness, decency, and bravery are available—not only to us but to all human beings." I was first attracted to this teaching because it was so counterintuitive. In this world of terrible and dehumanizing actions, wouldn't the most natural response be to feel angry, impotent, despairing? I expected that the more clearly I saw things, the angrier I would get. Of course this still happens, frequently. But I have learned that anger and despair will pass, if I let them. If I don't use negative emotions as motivation, if I refrain from feeling righteous about my anger, if I pause, these feelings move on. But they only leave when I consciously choose not to give them a hearing, not to develop a drama about what I just heard or saw.

In this culture of overreaction and constant judgment, it takes great discipline to refrain from creating made-in-the-moment dramas. Everyone else is, so why shouldn't we? Our only defense against this seduction is to be mindful, skilled at watching our reactions as quickly as possible.

If we can notice that we're caught up in emotions, then we can stop our story lines from blossoming into full-blown dramatic operas. If we can notice when we're getting angry or depressed or vengeful, such awareness gives us the ability to choose another response. Instead of justifying our anger, we can take time to calm down and select another reaction that would be more helpful in the situation. Instead of quickly seeking revenge, we could pause long enough to more fully understand the causes that led to another's offensive behavior. Pausing before reacting is the easiest way to shift from drama queen to warrior. The pause is so powerful because it gives us time to quiet the mind. And once we do, we discover that gentleness, decency and bravery are available.

They surface in the quiet mind because they have always been there. They are qualities of the human spirit, always present if we can get past the noise, fear, and fatigue of our everyday lives. How wonderful that we don't have to manufacture them or go to training programs to learn about them! They are right here, available to all people, what Chögyam Trungpa described as the wholesomeness and health that exist in all of us. We discover human goodness by acknowledging strong emotions when they appear, pausing, releasing our story lines, and then gratefully watching them pass away.[66] Once they pass, here we are, with just the capacities we need to be strong, useful warriors.

What I just described sounds so simple, but of course it takes a great deal of discipline not to get dragged down by these very strong and legitimate reactions to our world. Yet if we are to develop our skills as warriors, we need to be extremely well-disciplined, attending to our reactions and behaviors continuously.

Compassion Is Commonplace

Warriors have only two weapons at their disposal: compassion and insight. Of the two, compassion feels much simpler to access, because it is such a common trait, available in everyone. We don't have to insert it into people, we need only to create the conditions for it to surface. One of the easiest and best means for compassion to arise is in the basic human practice of talking to one another. I'm not referring to the shouting matches that are far too common these days, but to thoughtful, quiet conversations, where the rhetoric and "isms" dissolve and we begin to relate to each other as humans, just being. The more we listen, the more we recognize our common humanity, that we're all just humans sharing a common experience called life, no matter who we are or where we live. From that recognition, compassion naturally arises. It is always there, it just needs us to quiet down and become curious about one another.

Time after time in my own work, I've witnessed the delight of people as they discover each other in conversations. The room may be large, there may be many people there, but once they are in small-group conversations around meaningful topics, the chatter and noise subside and the space becomes beautifully quiet, filled with the lovely energy of discovery and connection. I know of no easier and more reliable way to experience human goodness, where our generous and compassionate selves eagerly engage with each other, than meaningful, slow conversations.

Compassion—literally meaning to suffer with—is a capacity we humans evolved as we learned that nothing living lives alone. Frans de Waal, a well-known primatologist (the study of monkeys, apes and humans), described us as "obligatorily gregarious," meaning that we have no alternative but to figure out how to live together.[67] We are a species with critical needs to belong and feel accepted. Every culture has worked with these needs, including today's global culture. Exile and invisibility have always been terrifying punishments. But as I mapped out in "Lost," the need to belong and feel accepted in the Internet world has driven us apart, creating lonely, grasping individuals increasingly narcissistic and paranoid. But still, compassion is in us, all of us. It takes dedicated warriors to remember this, to embody unshakable faith in human goodness, willing to create the conditions so that people again can discover that acting compassionately is a true source of meaning and delight—and the only path to survival.

Cultivating Basic Intelligence
Compassion is always present, no matter how deeply buried by fear and anger. But the warrior's second weapon, insight, takes years of discipline and practice to develop. Insight or discernment is the capacity to see clearly, to become aware of all the many elements and dynamics that are at play and then use that knowledge skillfully to find right action. We can't act skillfully if we can't see the situation fully. Absent clarity, we have no idea what's going on and just do what we've always done. As stress, fear, and distraction take over our lives, we lose treasured human capacities, as I hope I've made clear by now. Stressed people are creatures of habit who lack the capacity to choose a different response. They keep doing what they've always done, moving deeper into lostness without any means to recognize where they are. If we are to reawaken our brains and our precious human capacities, we have to create the conditions that support thinking and reflection. We have to actively cultivate insight through disciplined practice.

I haven't discovered any other means to develop insight except through a daily practice of quieting the mind, tuning in with all senses, being patient and open, just sitting, willing to watch thoughts come and go.[68] It needs to be a *daily* practice because the world is so crazy. We get pulled in contradictory directions by multiple demands; we get pummeled by fear-inducing reports; we move from task to task, gradually losing the capacity to think straight; we end up tired, perhaps uneasy, dissatisfied, frustrated. Perhaps too exhausted to even notice how we're feeling. And this is a normal day for many of us.

The world is spinning out of control. We can't expect the world to change, but we surely can. We can aspire to cultivate skillful means, knowing what to do and when to do it. We can commit to reclaiming our human intelligence. We can vow not to add to the fear and aggression of this world. If we aspire to any of these (and any one will lead to the others), we must find time for the practices that uncover our basic intelligence.

Just as we have natural goodness, we humans also have natural intelligence or sanity. It is inside us, where it has always been, just badly obscured by our distracted, frantic lives. Finding time to be with yourself—to watch your thoughts come and go for just ten minutes a day—develops the capacity to be aware of your reactions as you are out in the world dealing with your day. As we learn to be mindful, it is easier to be less reactive and more present; we don't get dragged off quite as fast by strong emotions. Watching our minds—whether in silent meditation, in a meeting, in traffic, or any high-stress place—it becomes possible to notice when we get "triggered" by a person or comment, when we suddenly find ourselves shifted from okay to angry, from open-hearted to hurt. And it becomes easier to notice how quickly we make up stories about others, filling the void of our ignorance about them with judgments and opinions.

What Triggers Me?

In this world of outrageous statements and behaviors, we have to expect that we will get triggered many times a day, even though our intention might be to remain calm and open. Rather than pretend that we are peaceful, imperturbable people, how much wiser it is to expect these vacillations between different emotional states, to prepare to be disturbed, frequently.

Over many years of practice, I've learned to identify some of my biggest triggers or hot buttons. I can go from zero to rage in a nanosecond when I hear certain phrases or get treated a certain way; for example, if anyone uses the phrase "those people" or speaks in a condescending voice to me or people I'm with, or if I'm standing in front of a store clerk who doesn't get off his cell phone. Even though I feel that my outrage is justifiable—people shouldn't talk about others or treat me in this way—noticing that I'm getting angry frees me from anger being the *only* reaction possible. If I notice it, I can let the anger pass and choose a different response, hopefully one that moves the situation forward in a more beneficial direction. (And one that supports me to honor my commitment not to add to the fear and aggression of this time.)

What I've just described takes a great deal of practice and willpower. And large doses of patience and forgiveness extended to one's self. The measure of success here is not that we stop getting provoked, but that we notice when it happens *sooner* and get over it *faster*. With a lot of practice, gradually the triggers fade away and it becomes easier to be less reactive and a more helpful presence for others.

I encourage you to notice your triggers—the predictable words, behaviors and situations that arouse instant and strong emotional responses. Since our physical bodies respond faster than our thoughts, some people notice they've been triggered because of an instant change in their bodies—face flushes, stomach tightens, head pounds. In whatever way your reactions show themselves, identifying triggers is a powerful lens to see how we've been conditioned, the inner workings of our minds. It can free us from habitual patterns; and it helps us become more peaceful and present people who don't get dragged down by knee-jerk emotional responses. (And do try this at home.)

I know of no one who is able to develop insight and compassion without a regular practice of quieting and watching the mind. And as the world's insanity continues to escalate, we have to do some form of mindfulness practice every day. We can no longer wait for weekends or vacations. As the university provost said, "Every day it's another psychotic event."

Maintaining Equanimity

As we become more knowledgeable about our triggers, we can develop the treasured state of equanimity—a quality of being open and alert to what we are seeing without instantly reacting to it. It isn't that we don't feel anything—in fact, we see and feel *more* when our hearts are open to the world. Our pain for the world is more acute and present than it is for most people. But the difference is that we don't let our emotions cloud our ability to see clearly; we don't lose our clarity in a fog of grief or sadness. We take in what is happening in great detail and therefore can figure out how best to respond, what would constitute right action.

Equanimity, like mindfulness, requires great diligence and much practice. Although I've been blessed to learn many practices for dealing with strong emotions and maintaining presence, still this world challenges my equanimity hour by hour. It takes extraordinary discipline to give up my anger when someone close to me suffers because of a new bureaucratic regulation, or a colleague's great project loses its funding, or a family member falls apart from stress, or a friend's boss tells her to lie to protect the organization.

I expect these things to occur every day now, but without a commitment to try to listen, pause, and not react instantly, I'd succumb to anger and despair. And I do succumb—in South Africa, I was so enraged while visiting a community destroyed by greed that I heard myself exclaiming that I'd be taking to the streets if I were young. And at a U.S. conference where someone described how corruption and greed were destroying lives and neighborhoods, I heard myself advocating for public hangings. I'm not proud of either of these statements, but at least I noticed where my anger led me. Perhaps next time I'll catch myself before I speak and not let anger derail me from my vow to refrain from adding to fear and aggression. At least I hope so.

A Genuine Heart of Sadness

Opening ourselves to the world as it is, not flinching from what we see, keeping our eyes and heart open—this is true warriors' work. And what we see will always break our hearts. It can't be otherwise. As Chögyam Trungpa described it: "When tenderness tinged by sadness touches our heart, we know that we are in contact with reality. We feel it. That contact is genuine, fresh and quite raw. That sensitivity is the basic experience of warriorship and it is the key to developing fearless renunciation [of our hard, aggressive, self-protective mentality]."[69]

Warriors need to expect to feel sad and oftentimes lonely because we see clearly a world that others deny. Yet many of us don't know what to do with our sadness and grief for the world. The more clearly we see what is going on, the more heartbroken we become. As poet Adrienne Rich wrote: "My heart is moved by all I cannot save, so much has been destroyed."[70] Perhaps we should suppress our grief and sorrow for fear that if we acknowledge them we will be unable to continue in our work. But there is another side to sadness.

Strangely but surely, sadness can also be the experience of joy. As we let our hearts be tenderized by this sorrow-filled world, we discover that joy and sadness are one, that we can't always distinguish between the two. Perhaps you have had this experience, of feeling tender and overwhelmed, heart wide open, vulnerable, overcome by tears of joy that also felt like sadness. In these moments of deep emotion, it doesn't matter that we can't define the feeling with simple words. We are inside the heart of a profound human experience, so very different from our everyday emotions.

Our challenge as warriors is not to be afraid of sadness, to let it in until our hearts are raw and open beyond recognition. As we do so, we may discover that it is possible to feel both grief-stricken and energized, fully aware of the darkness yet ever more joyful to be serving the human spirit.

The Brazilian theologian Rubem Alvez defined the source of discipline: "We must live by the love of what we will never see." Yet as I walk this path, I *do* see things that inspire me to maintain discipline. I see not only the pain and suffering, but the natural goodness, compassion and intelligence of people. Even though we're not going to save the world, we human beings are worth struggling for. And in the midst of all the struggle, there are still great pleasures to be found, especially moments of joy. There is joy because we humans are meant to be together, we are together, we were never separated. That was just a terrible optical delusion. In the worst times of loss and grief, when everything has been swept away, we're still here. We have not lost our compassion or intelligence. We're still together, just humans, being.

14

WARRIORS AT WORK

Warriors look like normal people.
Our true identity doesn't get revealed
by sudden costume changes.

To colleagues and family, It looks like we're still the same; going to meetings, filing reports, applying for grants, complying with regulations, teaching, healing, researching, leading. But inside, we've changed radically. We now work from different maps and expectations. We no longer think like most other people. We've recognized how lost we are, that no matter how hard we try, this world cannot be saved. We know that things will not calm down, that crises will not diminish, that leaders will not behave rationally, that global problems will not be resolved. We see clearly that there is no way out of the life-destroying cycles set in motion many years ago.

Yet we are not oppressed by this clarity. We've opened to the world as it is and discovered gentleness, decency, and bravery. We've discovered that humans are worth struggling for and can even be delightful company. We were invited to contemplate a new role for ourselves and accepted the invitation. Perhaps it felt natural to think of ourselves as warriors for the human spirit, perhaps it felt like a stretch, but here we are, looking just the same on the outside, transformed on the inside.

I've invited you into warriorship as if it were a conscious choice. But for most of us, this is choiceless. We have to accept this role, we can't *not* do it. And yet, as compelled as we might feel to be warriors, it's also true that we can easily get lost if we're not careful. Every day, incident by incident, we can find ourselves back in the familiar territory of anger, fear and aggression. The faster we work and the more overwhelmed we feel, the more at risk we are to slip back into old habits and outdated reactions. Warriorship requires new skills to navigate our way through this challenging territory, including such wonderful capacities as vigilance, confidence, equanimity, humor and true companionship.

A Map with New Signposts
One of my favorite quotes is: "If you don't know where you're going, any road will take you there." The warrior's path is unusual because it is not going anywhere, sometimes described as a path without a goal. We are not hoping to arrive somewhere; our only aspiration is to stay on the path itself. Thich Nhat Hahn describes this beautifully: "There is no way to peace. Peace is the way." In our earlier work, we knew where we were going and had maps to get us to a specific destination. We were going to create change, if not for the world then at least for the people, cause or community we were working with. We had measures, outcomes, goals, and we would know when we had arrived. That map kept getting more complicated, we kept getting lost, and, finally, we realized we were trapped in an impenetrable maze with no way out. We woke up to the fact that we needed a new map.

The map that guides warriors is very different from the usual map—it describes not the exterior world but our internal landscape. Warriors need to know *how* they are, not *where* they are. We already know where we are—we're lost. That's why we chose to become warriors. What we need from a map are signposts of how we're doing and what we're learning as we live guided by new aspirations. We have set some powerful aspirations in motion as baby warriors in training. We want to refrain from adding to the fear, aggression, and confusion of this time. We are eager to develop our skills of compassion and insight. We try every day to find opportunities to practice these nascent skills, no matter how challenging the situation.

As warriors in training, we have to let go of needing to be perfect. We have to expect to stumble and fall frequently as we take risks with new behaviors. As one leader commented after a devastating natural disaster, "We all took a lot of risks. But, in fact, there's no risk. It's already a disaster." In this already-a-disaster time, we need to encourage one another to experiment so that we learn how best to serve. And forgiveness plays a big role here. Let's not fall back into the old practice of beating ourselves up when we make mistakes.

The map we're relying on doesn't tell us anything about time. We have no idea if we'll ever arrive at our destination. We stop asking, "Are we there yet?" This path, our work, is endless. What we need to know is how well we are staying on the path, moment by moment, day by day, practicing our new skills, learning from our mistakes, becoming better warriors on the path without a goal.

Here is a practice I've found very helpful to keep me from getting lost in the bushes. If I remember to do this when I wake up (not always the case), I create a focus for the day: what behavior will I especially attend to today? What behavior will I seek opportunities to practice this day?

I learned this from a Tibetan teacher—each morning he chooses one behavior or quality he will focus on that day. Perhaps today he'll seek opportunities to practice forgiveness, or to be less reactive when provoked, or to be a better listener with his child. (A word of warning: be careful what opportunities for practice you ask for.) At the close of the day, just before sleep, he reflects on how he did. He is quick to emphasize that this self-assessment is *not* to blame or punish himself with guilt and remorse for what he failed to do well. Quite the opposite. He ends his reflection with expressions of gratitude and happiness directed toward himself. It doesn't matter whether he messed up— he is delighted and grateful that he is working to develop these qualities in himself.

Feeling happy with ourselves—quietly proud that we're willing to practice to become better warriors—is the most important part of this daily exercise, and the hardest to do for those of us skilled in self-recrimination. But as we practice being kind and loving to ourselves, we are learning how to be kind to others. Loving kindness is an essential skill for warriors and it begins at home.

Who Showed Up as Me Today?
Here are a few questions I use at the end of a day (you can infer the day's focus that I set that morning). I offer these as examples, not prescriptions; please make up your own. As you try out this practice, remember to choose only one behavior for the day and choose one that is doable that day. If it's a day when you feel strong and confident, choose one that is challenging; if it's a day when you feel exhausted or troubled, go easy on yourself and choose something really simple to accomplish. And most important, at the end of the day, after you've assessed how you did, give yourself a big thanks for being such a good

person, one brave enough to strive to develop these qualities and skills.

Examples of questions I've used:

- ~ How present was I for people today? What pulled me away from staying present?
- ~ How often did I get triggered today? Can I identify what those triggers are? Were there any new ones I could notice?
- ~ How good a listener was I today? Did I catch myself when I wasn't listening well? Did I refrain from interrupting or giving instant advice?
- ~ Where did I act aggressively today: wanting to get my own way; thinking of how to get back at someone; pushing through a crowd; swearing at a driver or news commentator?
- ~ How often did I act from true generosity, not wanting something in return?
- ~ Did I let fear get inside me today? How did I respond when I noticed the fear?
- ~ What behaviors would a stranger have observed in me today?

One last thing to note as we're keeping track of our behaviors: we must attend to our own well-being, not just the well-being of others. We need to notice how tired or frustrated we are, to know when it's time to take care of ourselves, when we need to leave the scene for a few minutes, hours or days. My personal signposts include noticing when I've become impatient, judgmental, and critical of others and/or myself. I've had to learn these the hard way, getting myself into a fair bit of trouble over the years, but now I know that the rising shriek of judgment means I'm tired, that I'm pushing too hard, that it's time to take a break. So I do. I have no desire to become Sisyphus ever again. I refuse to get back into boulder-rolling contests.

Restoring Thinking, Removing Randomness

Don Juan described the warrior's path as challenge after challenge. Warriors are different from other people because of how we relate to challenge. We accept it as a way of life. Because we expect challenges, whenever one appears we don't deny it, push it under the table, diminish its importance or simplify it. Instead, we get curious. Why is this problem appearing now? What might have been the multiple causes that created it? How many causes and key players can we identify? What do we know about them? How would we learn more about what provoked them to act as they did? And what do they need from this situation?

If we let curiosity guide us—rather than instant reactions and judgments—we become skilled in how to think about complex challenges. Taking time to think can be an unpopular position these days as people rush to find someone to blame and be done with it. But as we cultivate thinking and become aware of the many different causes that led to this current problem, it becomes impossible to go along with simplistic solutions or to participate in the search for scapegoats. Encouraging others to take time to be curious and thoughtful is important warrior's work. We are reintroducing clear thinking, reflection and understanding so that people can feel more competent. Restoring critical thinking makes it possible for people to shift from feeling like victims of randomness to becoming active participants in solving their complex challenges.

And unlike most people, warriors never assume that challenges will end, that after we solve this present one things will go smoothly. We know that things won't ever get back to normal; we gave up believing in normalcy a long time ago. To warriors, there is no such thing as "the new normal." We don't try to get comfortable with any one state and we don't fall into the trap of treating anything as permanent. Nothing stays the same for long. Change is just the way it is.

How Warriors Find Their Strength

We made a conscious decision when we chose this path. We exercised our freedom to take charge of the only thing in life under our control—our minds. We took responsibility for our actions and reactions, guided by the aspirations we set. We aspire to refrain from making things worse for people; we aspire not to add to the aggression and fear of this time; we aspire to be open and available to others. We long to be of service; we yearn to be those few people who exhibit sanity and peace. And as we do, people respond to us. They may not understand why they like being around us, but I've found that peace and sanity are natural magnetizers. No matter how loud they like their music or how busy they like their day, people respond to calm presence. When we can be that for others, we're introducing them to the possibility of their own sanity and peace. And we find increased energy and strength for our work.

Chögyam Trungpa described the strengths by which warriors develop and sustain their energy. I've loved working with these (see one version in *Perseverance*[71]). He taught that our strength grows as a consequence of our commitment to serve the world. With this strength, we can stay present for others in the most dark and difficult places and do our work with confidence and delight. On the surface, doesn't this seem implausible? We might be willing to work in the darkest places, but would we expect to feel delight at the opportunity? But as strange as this might seem, the experience of delight is one I've come to depend on.

I can easily recall the moments, recent and past, when I suddenly feel overwhelmed with delight and gratitude that I've been given the opportunity to do what I'm doing, no matter how harsh the external circumstances. For me, this is the visceral experience of right work; I feel strong and confident, happy to be right here, doing what I'm doing. I wonder if you've had these moments also? It is the delight of recognizing that we're exactly where we need to be, offering what is ours to give. How could we not experience delight and gratitude? How could we not confidently go into difficult places and look for more opportunities to be of service?

Of course, there are also those many moments when the voices of doubt and impotence surface. What am I doing here? Why did I ever get involved in this situation? I'm not the right person. I can't do anything. I'm a failure. I'm in over my head. How do I get out of this? It helps to expect these negative voices—they never go away completely. But we don't have to take them seriously. They're voices from the past not relevant to what we're doing now. Mindfulness again comes into play as the practice that supports us to silence our discouragement and doubt.

The practice for dealing with self-doubt is simple, but I find sometimes I have to repeat this practice over and over and over again. First, you notice that you've been taken captive by self-doubt, self-criticism, self-hatred. You acknowledge its presence. Then, either you ask it to leave (if you're feeling strong) or you just stop listening, practicing active ignorance. It is important *not* to create a story line at this point. Don't stop and ask *why* you're so hesitant or scared. If you do that, you'll be energizing the negative emotion just when you want it to leave. If you want it gone, you have to ignore it and just get on with your work. Ignore your thoughts and just keep doing what you've been doing. (If you have experience with Western psychology, you might recoil from this practice and want to probe the causes of self-doubt. However, this mindfulness practice corresponds to more recent developments in psychology and neuroscience—if you want to change your mind, first change your behavior.)

As we do our warrior's work, we gain strength and energy not from achieving results, but from keeping our hearts open, from our wholeheartedness. And I mean that term quite literally. As our hearts are wholly engaged, we experience ever more compassion for others, ever more confidence and energy that we can do our work. Our human hearts seem capable of infinite expansion when we find the work that is ours to do. And that's a delightful feeling.

What Were We Thinking?

Of course there are times when delight is a dim distant memory and we're exhausted and depressed. I won't forget the day when a dear friend, a woman who'd been working for years to create positive change, sat down next to me, let out a huge sigh, and said, "I know I accepted this role, I know I signed up for this work, but what was I thinking?" I remarked that her question would be a great title for the collective autobiography of all us activists. What were we thinking?

As warriors, we have to continually reaffirm to ourselves and each other why we are doing our work. We can't let our confidence and strength get eroded by the insanity we have to deal with every day, or by the constant harm we see being done to people and causes we cherish. We need each other, our small circle of other valiant ones. We can too easily lose our way if we don't stop for occasional conversations where we remember what first called to us, what we still love, where we find satisfaction however small and momentary. We need time together to comfort, support, and console one another.

And we also need time to let out our frustrations and despair through laughter, jokes, black humor. Some of my best memories of working in very hard places were the times we got into outrageously dark humor, sometimes for hours, not always with liquor involved. Humor lets us rise above the insanity and thus gain strength to return to it. I've started asking people I work with whether they've discovered this outlet. Rather guiltily, they admit to it. I like to hear this—it's a sign that they're preserving their mental health. If we can find the humor in all this darkness, it helps us not take everything so seriously or personally. It helps us go back into the craziness, reminded of how much we are needed as the bearers of sanity and peace.

And humor helps us maintain equanimity by dramatically lowering our expectations. Because we expect the world to make no sense, because we expect leaders to continue acting harmfully or stupidly, it becomes somewhat easier to accept the constant stream of evidence they provide us. We no longer expect sanity, except in ourselves.

I look forward to the day when I don't get shocked by whatever happens, no matter how awful. This is not because I want to be numb or callous, but because I want to maintain my equanimity and stay present. But truthfully, every time I think I've reached this point, something happens that stuns me. Can leaders really be as absurd as they appear to be? One of my favorite stories from the early years of quantum discoveries was from Werner Heisenberg, a founder of quantum theory. He described long, late night walks through Copenhagen where he kept asking himself, "Can nature possibly be so absurd as it seemed to us in these atomic experiments?"[72] His despairing question led somewhere good, to more discoveries and a new understanding of quantum reality. My similar question simply alerts me to the fact that I was still hoping that things wouldn't get any worse. As you'll read in the next essay, I regard hope as a serious problem.

Stop by Sometime
Earlier I called attention to how distracted we are, how our communication habits have deteriorated into texts and by-appointment-only phone calls. Here, I want to describe some truly radical behaviors for us warriors focused on how we communicate, fully aware of how much courage it takes to do these things. Here are a few radical acts: pick up the phone and call each other for no reason; drop in on each other; make it a priority to visit with one another in person.

Why am I advocating such radical acts? Simply because we have to create strong support for ourselves and each other. We know we can't persevere alone, we know we need each other, but then we get too casual about communicating with one another. As warriors, we can expect to be criticized, ignored, mocked, dismissed, invisible—this list should feel familiar by now. And we see the world differently than most; we can't share what we're seeing or feeling with many people. And most people, even those close to us, don't care about what we're doing. Loneliness is built into the warrior's job description—it's unavoidable. So we need each other.

"You Would Come, If Alive"

Years ago, when I was working for the Army Chief of Staff, Gordon Sullivan, he introduced me to the essence of warriorship by reading me a letter written at the end of the Civil War. It was a personal letter from General William T. Sherman to General Ulysses S. Grant, describing the reasons for their victory. General Sherman wrote, "I always knew you thought of me and that if I got in a tight place, you would come, if alive." I have yearned for this unequivocal support and have read this letter to many groups to encourage us to be more available to each other. We need to know that we're here for each other, that this is not a casual promise, that we won't ever let distraction keep us from each other. With my close colleagues, we pledge our support in today's terms: "If I see your name come up on my phone, I'll take the call." Not quite as stirring, but enough. I've worked with groups that have done the same—they put everyone's phone number (not emails) on speed dial with the pledge to answer immediately.

Let me suggest that we practice even greater bravery and drop in on colleagues or accost them wherever we see them. How else can we pierce through the distracted, superficial nature of communication? You'll worry that you're disturbing them. Of course you are. But you're worth it—you're offering the chance for a connection, a good old-fashioned conversation (not networking). In my own experience, after the first minute of wondering how long you're going to stand there, people settle in and begin to relish the opportunity to talk. Everyone is experiencing at least some distress and disconnect these days, and often it is more serious than that. A conversation in which at least one person is actively working to be present and stay calm (that would be you) is most welcome these days. We respond to any opportunity that makes us feel less alone. We humans really miss each other.

Through such a simple act as surprising someone with a conversation, we're demonstrating our faith as warriors for the human spirit. Beneath the façade of every distracted person there is compassion and intelligence waiting to break through the clutter of everyday life. Even if the individual doesn't know this, we do. The work of warriors is to remember who we are as humans and to make it possible for many people to rediscover how it feels to be fully human. We plunge open-hearted into this world of confusion, aggression, and greed, inviting challenge, practicing discernment, accepting change and uncertainty, coping with despair and exhaustion. And from it all, we find rich lives overflowing with meaning and delight because the human spirit is always worth the struggle.

15

NO HOPE NO FEAR

Many years ago, I was introduced to a phrase that both intrigued and confused me. It is a familiar phrase in Buddhist texts: "the place beyond hope and fear," a state of awareness that frees us from suffering.

In today's global culture, where we're incessantly told to strive for achievement and success, to be positive and hopeful, why would we ever want to give up hope? It seems incomprehensible that this would be a good thing. After all, Dante defined Hell by writing, "Abandon all hope, ye who enter herein."

Nowadays, we live and breathe hope. It doesn't matter what religion you were raised in, hope plays a central role, often being the very essence of the faith—hope for heaven, for redemption, for peace, for a good life, for something better than what we have now. The prophets in the Old Testament warned, "Without vision, the people perish." And of course they're right. People who lose hope lose their life energy and die, at least spiritually and emotionally. So why would we ever want to give up hope?

At the very start of this book (I do not expect you to remember this), I spoke of hope as "an ambush," as one of my teachers describes it. Ambushes offer something so enticing that the animals can't resist. They just have to have it. They walk into the trap, become ensnared, then get carried away to be eaten. Think about how much hope entices and motivates you to do your work. You hope to change things, you hope to have an impact, you hope to work hard and get results, you hope to be rewarded for your dedicated work. Hope is irresistible, just like any good bait. But we need to see hope for what it is, a desire that ensnares us and ultimately robs us of energy to do our work. Hope can even be life threatening, as described in the "Stockdale Paradox."

The "Stockdale Paradox" was coined by business author Jim Collins after he interviewed Admiral James Stockdale, the highest-ranking officer ever to be imprisoned, held for seven years in a Vietnamese POW camp in extremely harsh and tortuous conditions.[73] Stockdale reported that he "never lost faith in the end of the story," that he believed he would prevail, that he would later see this horror as the defining event of his life. Those who didn't survive, he emphasized, were the *optimists*, those who believed they'd be out of prison by a certain date. As each date passed and they were still imprisoned, they gave up and died, in his words, "from broken hearts." Stockdale understood why they died: "You must never confuse faith that you will prevail in the end—which you can never afford to lose—with the discipline to confront the most brutal facts of your current reality, whatever they might be."[74]

I wonder if you're starting to be disturbed by these comments about hope and the problem of optimism. If you've grown up in this hope-filled culture or listened to a lot of motivational speakers, it is extremely difficult to look at the dark side of hope. But I encourage you to stay in this inquiry with me, because my intention is to free you from the ambush of hope and offer a much more sustainable source of energy for your work, the place beyond hope and fear.

The South African Flip

South Africans were famous for their hope. In any conversation, I'd wait for the moment when they visibly would flip into hope. That's what it felt like, a flip. They'd be describing the complexity of the issue they were working on, analyzing it from all directions, displaying real skills at systems analysis. I still admire their capacity to think in terms of multiple causes. After these complex descriptions, we'd all start to feel on the verge of despair given the enormity of the problems. And then they'd flip. They'd brighten up, a light would come into their eyes, and they'd emphatically declare that they had hope, they knew it was possible to solve these problems. Many people have remarked on this experience. I always loved listening to them and, at that time, I too believed that hope would conquer all. And then hope began disappearing from South African voices—I noticed this between trips there in 2005 and 2007. As I described earlier, people are still doing their very good work but, at least for my friends and colleagues, they no longer believe it will make a significant difference. Instead, they feel they have no choice but to keep going, to keep doing what they can to serve the people in front of them. But dreams of a new nation birthed by hopeful, tireless people have dissipated.

Yet this is not a story of defeat. These South Africans have discovered the place beyond hope, which is also the place beyond fear. Strange as it may seem, because they are no longer ambushed by hope, they are fearless. And this is what the ancient texts were saying. When there is no hope, there is no fear, because hope and fear are two sides of the same coin. We may have thought that hope made us fearless, giving us the strength to persevere. But hope is always and forever accompanied by its marriage partner, fear. If we hope that something will happen, we fear that it won't.

We've all had this experience many times. We worked day and night to accomplish something, propelled by the hope of success, and then it fell apart or our funding was withdrawn. Or we hoped that change was coming with new leadership, and then it didn't. If you look at your own experience, you'll be able to see the intimate partnership between hope and fear. It's always there, a roller-coaster ride through life, excited then disappointed, exhilarated then scared, hopeful then fearful. Hope creates inspiring dreams, then fear of failing robs our energy. Hope pushes us to keep going to the breaking point, fear then tells us we're a failure.

If giving up hope still seems hard for you, how would you feel if you could give up fear? What would it feel like for you to be fearless? Perhaps that might motivate your exploration of the place beyond hope and fear.

Hope Is the Essence of Being Human
I've been contemplating the place beyond hope and fear for several years now and written about it many times. I was pushed into this contemplation years ago when one of my teachers asked me to give up saving the world. She asked this to help liberate me from hope and fear, but I couldn't see that then. I went into a deep depression, feeling as though I had lost the love of my life. I felt I was destroying my life's purpose and I couldn't imagine how the world would be saved without me (really). None of my colleagues and friends admired my decision to give

up saving the world—many of them accused me of being irresponsible, selfish, depressed. But because I trusted my teacher's guidance, I disciplined myself to give up hoping that my work would bear fruit. It has taken years, but now I do know what is available the other side of hope and fear. It is clear-seeing, right work, commitment, energy, strength, perseverance, love—all the warrior skills you've been reading about here.

And yet, there is something to what we call "hope" that I would never abandon. I've looked for words to describe this and the closest I've come is "the essence of being human." I learned this from Václav Havel, poet, playwright, leader of the Velvet Revolution and then first president of the Czech Republic: "Hope is a dimension of the soul . . . an orientation of the spirit, an orientation of the heart. It transcends the world that is immediately experienced and is anchored somewhere beyond its horizons."

This extraordinary statement describes who we humans are, the nature of our human spirits. Hope is not a feeling that comes and goes with external circumstances. Hope is who we are independent of outcomes. Hope is as basic to humans as compassion and intelligence. It is always present, it never leaves us. It is not dependent on success and not afflicted by failure. Thus, it is free from fear. And without fear, we can see clearly. We see what our work is, we have the strength to persevere, we do what we feel is right work and, as poet T. S. Eliot wrote, "the rest is not our business."

And freed from hope and fear, we give up needing to save the world. With a sigh of relief. We discover that abandoning our cause has freed us to work with even greater dedication and energy, not because we'll accomplish great things but because we've claimed our right work. As

Havel also said: "Hope, in this deep and powerful sense, is not the same as joy that things are going well, or willingness to invest in enterprises that are obviously heading for success, but rather an ability to work for something because it is good, not just because it stands a chance to succeed."[75]

Your Work Will Be Apparently Worthless

I've also been deeply affected by a letter written by Thomas Merton, the famed Christian mystic, activist and author to a friend despairing over the failure of his work. Merton wrote, "Do not depend on the hope of results . . . you may have to face the fact that your work will be apparently worthless and even achieve no result at all, if not perhaps results opposite to what you expect. As you get used to this idea, you start more and more to concentrate not on the results, but on the value, the rightness, the truth of the work itself. . . . You gradually struggle less and less for an idea and more and more for specific people. . . . In the end, it is the reality of personal relationship that saves everything."[76]

I've read this letter to thousands of people over the years; most people find it very challenging. Merton stands normal career coaching on its head: your work is worthless, it won't be successful, and it might actually create more harm. Certainly no hope being offered there. But hasn't this been true in your experience? You work hard for something, then it not only fails but causes problems for people, much to your chagrin. Certainly you didn't intend to cause harm, but in this densely tangled web of relationships, we have to expect creating results opposite to what we intended. We never know what's going to happen as our work moves through entanglements.

Merton consoles us with his clarity about what's truly important in life, which is our relationships. No matter how despairing the circumstance, it is our relationships that offer us comfort, guidance, and joy. As long as we're together, as long as we feel others supporting us, we can persevere. I have learned this many times over working with people and communities who've been uprooted by wars, hurricanes, famines, dictators. No matter what tragedy people are experiencing, their suffering is alleviated when they learn that others are standing with them. Some of my best teachers of this truth have been younger leaders. One in her twenties said, "*How* we're going is important, not where. I want to go together and with faith." A young Danish woman at the end of a conversation that moved us all to despair, quietly spoke: "I feel like we're holding hands as we walk into a deep, dark woods." A Zimbabwean, in her darkest moment, wrote, "In my grief I saw myself being held, us all holding one another in this incredible web of loving kindness. Grief and love in the same place. I felt as if my heart would burst with holding it all."

I've witnessed this so many times that I know we humans can get through anything as long as we're together. Thomas Merton was right. We are consoled and strengthened by being together. We don't need specific outcomes. We don't need hope. We need each other. And as we share our common journey, careful to stay together, we discover that hope has never left us. It is the essence of being human, always present just beyond the horizon of events and difficulties. And so we keep moving forward, free from hope and fear, confident that we have found our right work, developing our skillful means with discipline and delight.

A PATH FOR WARRIORS

We are grateful to discover our right work
and happy to be engaged in it.

We embody values and practices that offer us meaningful
lives now. We let go of needing to impact the future.

We refrain from adding to the aggression,
fear, and confusion of this time.

We welcome every opportunity to practice our skills
of compassion and insight, even very challenging ones.

We resist seeking the illusory comfort of certainty
and stability.

We delight when our work achieves good results
yet let go of needing others to adopt our successes.

We know that all problems have complex causes.
We do not place blame on any one person or cause,
including ourselves and colleagues.

We are vigilant with our relationships, mindful to
counteract the polarizing dynamics of this time.

Our actions embody our confidence that humans can get
through anything as long as we're together.

We stay present to the world as it is with open minds and hearts,
knowing this cultivates our gentleness, decency, and bravery.

We care for ourselves as tenderly as we care for others,
taking time for rest, reflection, and renewal.

We are richly blessed with moments of delight, humor,
grace, and joy. We are grateful for these.

A DREAM OF WARRIORS

Inspired by a dream of Thich Nhat Hahn's

They were exhausted. They had been traveling longer than they could remember. Their journey had begun with energy and enthusiasm, but that too they could no longer recall. They had lost many companions along the way— some had turned back, some had refused to go on, some had died of weariness. They all had suffered greatly.

They came to a narrow bridge that spanned a great river running swift and fast. On the far shore they could see what they had dreamed of during all these years of hardship—gentle green valleys and peaceful lakes reflecting clear blue sky. They stood there, astonished to realize that what they had struggled so long for was suddenly here.

They began walking across the bridge with joyful steps. Midway across, they were stopped by children who had come to meet them. Tears overcame them for their own children left behind long ago. The children began to speak: "You cannot enter our land. You must go back. You will need to repeat your struggles. You must go back and do it all again."

The warriors stood there quietly. They gazed longingly at the pleasant pastures. They beheld the bright faces of the children. Tenderly, they bent down and kissed their cheeks. Then they stood up and spoke: "We are not afraid." And they turned back, to begin again their journey.

Notes

An Invitation to Warriorship

1. Namkhai Norbu, *The Mirror* (a publication of the Dzogchen Community, Conway, MA), 113 (November–December 2011): 2.

2. Joanna Macy's description, from her teacher, Dugu Choegyal, of the Tashi Jong community in northwestern India. In *Active Hope: How to Face the Mess We're in Without Going Crazy* (Novato, CA: New World Library, 2012), 101–102.

Chapter 1
Seeing What Is

3. See my book, *Perseverance* (San Francisco: Berrett-Koehler, 2010), organized around this prophecy.

4. *Long Walk to Freedom* is the title of Nelson Mandela's autobiography, a good part of it written while he was imprisoned on Robben Island.

5. Václav Havel, *Disturbing the Peace: A Conversation with Karel Hvizdala*, trans. Paul Wilson (New York: Vintage Books, 1990), 181.

Chapter 2
Do You Want to Save the World?

6. Chögyam Trungpa, *Shambhala: The Sacred Path of the Warrior,* ed. Carolyn Rose Gimian (Boston: Shambhala Publications, 1988), 133.

7. Desmond and Mpho Tutu, *Made for Goodness: And Why This Makes All the Difference* (London: Rider, 2010), 104.

Chapter 4
Everything Comes from Somewhere

8. As complexity scientist Stuart Kauffman frequently describes it. See Wheatley and Kellner-Rogers, *A Simpler Way* (San Francisco: Berrett-Koehler, 1996), 31.

Chapter 5
Emergence: Surprised by Newness

9. Margaret Wheatley, *Leadership and the New Science: Discovering Order in an Orderly Universe*, 3rd ed. (San Francisco: Berrett-Koehler, 2006), 119.

Chapter 6
Identity: The Logic of Change

10. Ibid., 81.

11. Sharon Begley, *Train Your Mind, Change Your Brain: How a New Science Reveals Our Extraordinary Potential to Transform Ourselves* (New York: Random House, Kindle Edition, 2008), 10.

12. Nicolas Carr, *The Shallows: How the Internet Is Changing Our Brains* (New York: Norton, 2011), 121.

13. Richard C. Francis, *Epigenetics: The Ultimate Mystery of Inheritance* (New York: Norton, Kindle Edition, 2011), 19.

14. "Why Your DNA Isn't Your Destiny," *Time,* January 10, 2012, www.time.com/time/magazine/article/0,9171,1952313,00 .html#ixzz1lO1EOG5S (accessed April 7, 2012).

15. Sherry Turkel, *Alone Together: Why We Expect More from Technology and Less from Each Other* (New York: Basic Books, 2011), 183.

16. Ibid., 183.

Chapter 7
Relationships: Endlessly Entangled

17. Albert Einstein, *The New Quotable Einstein*, ed. Alice Calaprice (Princeton, NJ: Princeton University Press, 2005), 206. A letter dated February 12, 1950, "to a distraught father who had lost his young son and had asked Einstein for some comforting words." Two different versions of this letter have been printed. This is the more popular one, printed in the *New York Times*, March 29, 1972. See http://en.wikiquote.org/ wiki/Albert_Einstein (accessed April 6, 2012).

18. Dean Radin, *Entangled Minds: Experiences in a Quantum Reality* (New York: Simon & Schuster, Kindle Edition 2009), 14.

19. Wheatley, *Leadership and the New Science*, 33.

20. Radin, *Entangled Minds*, 131.

21. Ibid., 231.

22. Margaret Wheatley and Deborah Frieze, *Walk Out Walk On: A Learning Journey into Communities Daring to Live the Future Now* (San Francisco: Berrett-Koehler, 2011), 141–142.

23. Ibid., 81–82.

24. Radin, *Entangled Minds*, 36.

25. Kerr, Jessica, "To Live Is to Know," *Holistic Science Journal* 1, issue 3 (July 2011): 31.

26. Wheatley, *Leadership and the New Science*, 35.

27. Turkel, *Alone Together*, 203.

28. Ibid., 187–209.

29. Ibid., 203.

30. David Riesman, Nathan Glazer, and Reuel Denney, *The Lonely Crowd: A Study of the Changing American Character,* originally published in 1950 (New Haven, CT: Yale University Press, 2001).

31. Turkel, *Alone Together,* 11–12.

32. Ibid., 10.

33. Meteorologist Ed Lorenz coined the term from his original research; see Wheatley, *Leadership and the New Science*, 121.

Chapter 8
Are We Lost?

34. Laurence Gonzales, *Deep Survival: Who Lives, Who Dies, and Why* (New York: Norton, 2005), 166–167, 240.

Chapter 9
All-Consuming Selves

35. John Muir, *My First Summer in the Sierra* (Boston: Houghton Mifflin, 1911), 110.

36. Carr, *The Shallows*, 217.

37. Ibid., 159.

38. National Public Radio, *Science Friday* broadcasts, "Five Conspiracy Theories About Climate Change," November 2011.

39. Shawn Lawrence Otto, *Fool Me Twice: Fighting the Assault on Science in America* (Emmaus, PA: Rodale, Kindle Edition, 2011), 6-7.

40. Ibid., 5.

41. Gary Snyder, "For the Children," in Wheatley, *Turning to One Another*, 2nd ed. (San Francisco: Berrett-Koehler, 2009), 17.

Chapter 10
Distracted Beyond Recall

42. Joanna Macy and Chris Johnstone, *Active Hope: How to Face the Mess We're in Without Going Crazy* (Novato CA: New World Library, 2012), 145.

43. T. S . Eliot, "Four Quartets," in Carr, *The Shallows*, 121.

44. Carr, *The Shallows,* 91.

45. See http://en.wikipedia.org/wiki/Jacques_Ellul (accessed February 10, 2012).

46. Jacques Ellul and William H. Vanderburg, *Perspectives on Our Age: Jacques Ellul Speaks on His Life and Work* (New York: Perseus Books, Kindle Edition, 2011), 32.

47. Carr, *The Shallows,* 4.

48. John Brockman, ed., *Is the Internet Changing the Way You Think? The Net's Impact on Our Minds and Future* (New York: Harper Perennial, 2011), 104.

49. Carr, *The Shallows,* 125.

50. Ibid., 131.

51. Ibid., 118.

52. Ibid., 141.

53. Choegyal Namkhai Norbu, *The Precious Vase* (Arcidosso, Italy: Shang Shung, 1999), 26.

Chapter 11
Controlling Complexity

54. See Wheatley, *Leadership and the New Science.*

55. See Wheatley and Kellner-Rogers, *A Simpler Way.*

56. Michael Lewis, *The Big Short: Inside the Doomsday Machine* (New York: Norton, Kindle Edition, 2010), Chapter 10, "Accidental Capitalists."

57. Personal notes taken at a public talk by Taleb, summer 2009.

58. In April 2011, Senator Jon Kyl, Republican-AZ (recognized by *Time* magazine as one of the one hundred most influential people in the world for his persuasive role in the Senate) publicly stated that Planned Parenthood used "well over 90%" of its funds for abortions. In fact, they spend only 3 percent. When challenged on this point, his office replied, "His remark was not intended to be a factual statement, but rather to illustrate that Planned Parenthood, an organization that receives millions of dollars in taxpayer funding, does subsidize abortions." This story was widely covered in the press. See http://www.huffingtonpost.com/2011/04/08/jon-kyl-is-sorry-if-he-ga_n_846941.html (accessed April 7, 2012)

59. Notes from a personal conversation with the author, January 2012.

60. See the film *Inside Job,* released fall 2010, www.sony classics.com/insidejob/.

61. Gretchen Morgenson and Joshua Rosner, *Reckless Endangerment: How Outsized Ambition, Greed, and Corruption Led to Economic Armageddon* (New York: Holt, 2011), xv.

62. Nassim Nicholas Taleb, *The Black Swan: The Impact of the Highly Improbable,* 2nd ed. (New York: Random House, Kindle Edition, 2010), location 7618.

63. Morgenson and Rosner, *Reckless Endangerment: How Outsized Ambition, Greed, and Corruption Led to Economic Armageddon,* xiv.

Chapter 12
A Prophecy of Warriors
64. Macy and Johnstone, *Active Hope*, 101–102.

Chapter 13
Choosing for the Human Spirit
65. Chogyam Trungpa, *Smile at Fear*, p. 8

66. For a richer description of this and other very helpful practices, see Pema Chödrön, *Taking the Leap: Freeing Ourselves from Old Habits and Fears* (Boston: Shambhala Publications, 2009).

67. Desmond and Mpho Tutu, *Made for Goodness: And Why That Matters* (London: Rider, 2010), 14.

68. For a wonderful guide to meditation practice, see Sharon Salzburg, *Real Happiness: The Power of Meditation: A 28-Day Program* (New York: Workman, 2010).

69. Chögyam Trungpa, Carolyn Gimian, ed., *Smile at Fear: Awakening the True Heart of Bravery* (Boston: Shambhala Publications, 2009), 58.

70. Adrienne Rich, in Wheatley and Frieze, *Walk Out Walk On*, 218.

Chapter 14
Warriors at Work

71. Margaret Wheatley, *Perseverance* (San Francisco: Berrett-Koehler, 2010), 147.

72. Wheatley, *Leadership and the New Science*, 6.

Chapter 15
No Hope, No Fear

73. Jim Collins audio at http://www.jimcollins.com/media_topics/brutal-facts.html (accessed April 8, 2012).

74. Quoted by Jim Collins, http://en.wikipedia.org/wiki/James_Stockdale - cite_note-9 (accessed April 8, 2012).

75. Václav Havel, *Disturbing the Peace*, 181.

76. Thomas Merton, a letter written to James Forest, February 21, 1966. In *The Hidden Ground of Love: Letters by Thomas Merton on Religious Experience and Social Concerns,* ed. William Shannon (New York: Farrar, Strauss, Giroux, 1993).

Index

daily focus of, 143–145
dream of, 166
equanimity of, 136–137, 150
for human spirit, 10–12, 50,
  129–139, 141
maps guiding, 17, 142–143
path for, 163–164
in place beyond hope and
  fear, 155–161
prophecy of, 125–126
role of, 10, 18, 141–142
sadness of, 137–139
self-doubt of, 148–149
Shambhala, 125
strength and energy of,
  147–149
supporting other colleagues,
  151–153
at work, 141–153

Work
  meaningful, 113
  of warriors, 141–153
  as worthless, 160–161
World
  accepting realities of, 11
  acknowledgment of negative
    forces in, 69–72
  chaos and randomness in,
    99–100
  destructive forces in, 24,
    70–71
  global culture of. *See* Global
    culture
  hope for saving, 4, 9–10

Yeats, W. B., 4, 78

Photo Credits

All photos by Margaret Wheatley except photo Part IV, p. 122.

Cover Photo   Zion National Park, Utah

About the Author

Margaret (Meg) Wheatley, Ed.D., writes, teaches, and speaks about how we can organize and accomplish our work in chaotic times, sustain our relationships, and willingly step forward to serve. Since 1973, Meg has worked with an unusually broad variety of organizations: Her clients and audiences range from the head of the U.S. Army to twelve-year-old Girl Scouts, from CEOs and government ministers to small-town ministers, from large universities to rural aboriginal villages. All of these organizations and people wrestle with a common dilemma—how to maintain their integrity, focus, and effectiveness as they cope with the relentless upheavals and rapid shifts of this troubling time. But there is another similarity: a common human desire to find ways to live together more harmoniously, more humanely, so that more people may benefit.

She has written several best-selling books: *Walk Out Walk On: A Learning Journey into Communities Daring to Live the Future Now*, coauthored with Deborah Frieze (2011); *Perseverance* (2010); *Leadership and the New Science* (eighteen languages and third edition); *Turning to One Another: Simple Conversations to Restore Hope to the Future* (seven languages and second edition); *Finding Our Way: Leadership for an Uncertain Time;* and *A Simpler Way* (coauthored with Myron Kellner-Rogers). Her numerous articles appear in both professional and popular journals and may be downloaded free from her website.

Meg earned her doctorate in organizational behavior from Harvard University and a master's in Media Ecology from New York University. She also studied at University College London, England. She has been a global citizen since her youth, serving in the Peace Corps in Korea in the 1960s, and has taught, consulted, or served in an advisory capacity on all continents (except Antarctica). She began her career as a public school teacher and urban educator. She has been a full-time professor in two graduate management programs (Brigham Young University and Cambridge College, Massachusetts).

She is cofounder and president of The Berkana Institute, founded in 1991. Berkana has been a leader in experimenting with new organizational forms based on a coherent theory of living systems. Berkana has worked in partnership with a rich diversity of people around the world who strengthen their communities by working with the wisdom and wealth already present in their people, traditions and environment. These pathfinders do not deny or flee from our global crisis. Instead, they respond by moving courageously into the future now, experimenting with many different solutions.

Meg has received several awards and honorary doctorates. In 2003, the American Society for Training and Development (ASTD) honored her for her contribution "to workplace learning and development" and dubbed her "a living legend." In April 2005, she was elected to the Leonardo da Vinci Society for the Study of Thinking for her contribution to the development of the field of systems thinking. In 2010, she was appointed by the White House and the Secretary of the Interior to serve on the National Advisory Board of the National Parks System; her primary responsibility is to support the growth of a twenty-first-century culture of adaptation and innovation throughout the system of nearly 400 national parks.

She returns from her frequent global travels to her home in the mountains of Utah and the true peace of wilderness. She has raised a large family now dispersed throughout the United States and is a very happy mother and grandmother.

> **www.margaretwheatley.com** contains a rich treasure trove of articles, podcasts, and video clips that may be downloaded for free. Also on her website you can purchase her DVDs, Conversation Starter Kits, and other products.

Also by Margaret J. Wheatley

paintings by Asante Salaam

Perseverance

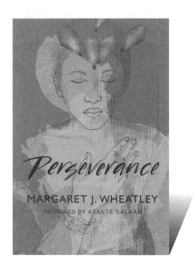

If we commit to a new role as *warriors for the human spirit*,
where do we find the strength and skillful means to persevere?
How do we serve the people, places, and causes we most care
about, even as we meet with setbacks, exhaustion, and frustration? In this series of brief, graceful essays, Margaret Wheatley
offers a gentle guide for how we can deal well with familiar experiences such as anger, criticism, exhaustion, jealousy—the many
emotions that rob us of energy and capacity. She places each in
a broader human or timeless perspective, offering ways for us to
act wisely and continue in our work with stamina and even joy.
Perseverance features poems and quotations drawn from traditions and cultures around the world and throughout history, thus
providing deep spiritual grounding.

Paperback, 168 pages, ISBN 978-1-60509-820-3
PDF ebook, ISBN 978-1-60509-854-8

Berrett–Koehler Publishers, Inc.
San Francisco, *www.bkconnection.com*   **800.929.2929**

Margaret Wheatley and Deborah Frieze

Walk Out Walk On
A Learning Journey into Communities Daring to Live the Future Now

In this era of intractable problems and shrinking resources, can we find meaningful and enduring solutions to the challenges we face today as individuals, neighborhoods, and nations? Margaret Wheatley and Deborah Frieze invite you on a learning journey to seven communities around the world to meet people who have *walked out* of limiting beliefs and assumptions and *walked on* to create healthy and resilient communities.

Paperback, 288 pages, ISBN 978-1-60509-731-2
PDF ebook, ISBN 978-1-60509-732-9

Margaret J. Wheatley

Leadership and the New Science
Discovering Order in a Chaotic World, 3rd Edition

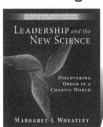

In this acclaimed and influential bestseller, Margaret Wheatley describes how recent discoveries in biology, chaos theory, and quantum physics radically alter our understanding of the world and can teach us how to live and work well together in these chaotic times. She combines science with real-world examples of how organizations are complex networks of interdependent relationships and the leadership they require.

Paperback, 240 pages, ISBN 978-1-57675-344-6
PDF ebook, ISBN 978-1-60509-147-1

Berrett–Koehler Publishers, Inc.
San Francisco, *www.bkconnection.com*   **800.929.2929**

Turning to One Another

Simple Conversations to Restore Hope to the Future, 2nd Edition

Real social change will not come from governments or corporations, Margaret Wheatley argues, but from the ageless process of thinking together in conversation. Through essays, images, and quotes, she sets the conditions for genuine, thoughtful exchanges and then provides ten "conversation starters"—questions that in her experience have led people to share their deepest beliefs, fears, and hopes.

Paperback, 192 pages, ISBN 978-1-57675-764-2
PDF ebook, ISBN 978-1-57675-984-4

Finding Our Way

Leadership for an Uncertain Time

In this collection of Margaret Wheatley's practice-focused articles, she applies themes she has addressed throughout her career to detail the organizational practices and behaviors that bring them to life. *Finding Our Way* sums up her thinking on a diverse scope of topics, from leadership and management to social change and our personal role in these turbulent times, from provocative social commentary to specific organizational practices, and more.

Paperback, 312 pages, ISBN 978-1-57675-405-4
Hardcover, ISBN 978-1-57675-317-0
PDF ebook, ISBN 978-1-60509-146-4

BK Berrett–Koehler Publishers, Inc.
San Francisco, *www.bkconnection.com*   **800.929.2929**

Berrett–Koehler
Publishers

Berrett-Koehler is an independent publisher dedicated to an ambitious mission: *Creating a World That Works for All*.

We believe that to truly create a better world, action is needed at all levels—individual, organizational, and societal. At the individual level, our publications help people align their lives with their values and with their aspirations for a better world. At the organizational level, our publications promote progressive leadership and management practices, socially responsible approaches to business, and humane and effective organizations. At the societal level, our publications advance social and economic justice, shared prosperity, sustainability, and new solutions to national and global issues.

A major theme of our publications is "Opening Up New Space." Berrett-Koehler titles challenge conventional thinking, introduce new ideas, and foster positive change. Their common quest is changing the underlying beliefs, mindsets, institutions, and structures that keep generating the same cycles of problems, no matter who our leaders are or what improvement programs we adopt.

We strive to practice what we preach—to operate our publishing company in line with the ideas in our books. At the core of our approach is stewardship, which we define as a deep sense of responsibility to administer the company for the benefit of all of our "stakeholder" groups: authors, customers, employees, investors, service providers, and the communities and environment around us.

We are grateful to the thousands of readers, authors, and other friends of the company who consider themselves to be part of the "BK Community." We hope that you, too, will join us in our mission.

A BK Life Book

This book is part of our BK Life series. BK Life books change people's lives. They help individuals improve their lives in ways that are beneficial for the families, organizations, communities, nations, and world in which they live and work. To find out more, visit **www.bk-life.com**.

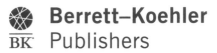

Berrett–Koehler
Publishers

A community dedicated to creating
a world that works for all

Visit Our Website: www.bkconnection.com

Read book excerpts, see author videos and Internet movies, read
our authors' blogs, join discussion groups, download book apps, find
out about the BK Affiliate Network, browse subject-area libraries of
books, get special discounts, and more!

Subscribe to Our Free E-Newsletter, the *BK Communiqué*

Be the first to hear about new publications, special discount offers,
exclusive articles, news about bestsellers, and more! Get on the list
for our free e-newsletter by going to **www.bkconnection.com**.

Get Quantity Discounts

Berrett-Koehler books are available at quantity discounts for orders
of ten or more copies. Please call us toll-free at (800) 929-2929 or
email us at bkp.orders@aidcvt.com.

Join the BK Community

BKcommunity.com is a virtual meeting place where people from
around the world can engage with kindred spirits to create a world
that works for all. **BKcommunity.com** members may create their own
profiles, blog, start and participate in forums and discussion groups,
post photos and videos, answer surveys, announce and register for
upcoming events, and chat with others online in real time. Please join
the conversation!

Certified Sourcing
www.sfiprogram.org
SFI-00453

Certified

Corporation
bcorporation.net